EFFORTLESS LIVING

"Immersing yourself in the origins and underpinnings of this ancient way of thinking and being will definitely help usher you into the Intuition Age with its interconnected, holographic perception. This book is brimming over with gems and overall wisdom. It's a comprehensive weaving of many threads that makes for a fascinating—and useful—read."

PENNEY PEIRCE, AUTHOR OF *LEAP OF PERCEPTION*
AND *FREQUENCY*

"In the West, people say, 'where there's a will there's a way,' by imposing your will over nature. More often than not this backfires. In ancient China, the wise ones discovered that the best way is *wu-wei,* 'doing nothing,' and thereby getting everything done by letting nature take its course. In this book you'll learn how that's not-done."

DANIEL REID, AUTHOR OF *THE TAO OF HEALTH, SEX,
AND LONGEVITY* AND *THE TAO OF DETOX*

"In *Effortless Living,* Jason Gregory explains in clear and simple terms the Taoist concept of wu-wei and reintroduces a model of contemplation much needed in the world today. He describes how wu-wei (literally 'not forcing' or 'allowing') can facilitate communion with the Tao—the timeless flow from which everything else we perceive is but a reflection. I thoroughly enjoyed this book, and I learned so much from it. My humble thanks to Jason Gregory for facilitating my own understanding of the Tao and, in doing so, allowing me to apprehend the inner silence and to listen to its wordless wisdom."

ANTHONY PEAKE, AUTHOR OF *THE INF   ͏͏ΈLD* AND *OPENING THE
DOORS OF PERCEPTION* AND   MIND

"Jason Gregory has tapped into a living   anti-
dote to our cultural numbness. By lea   than
interfere and intervene in an unnatural order of   love
the world again, by trusting it. This is essential and practical w   for a
modern social world at its best."

KINGSLEY L. DENNIS, AUTHOR OF *THE PHOENIX GENERATION*
AND *NEW CONSCIOUSNESS FOR A NEW WORLD*

"*Effortless Living* is a timely book. In a time where absolutist and rigid views are proving to be outmoded if not dangerous, Jason Gregory uses his heart and critical thinking skills to lay bare the essential, irreducible teachings of Lao-tzu. He deconstructs the myths, formulaic thinking, and the business of ritual of Taoism as it is practiced today that obscure and often hinder our innate abilities to have a direct experience of that from which we are never separate."

ROBERT SACHS, AUTHOR OF *THE PASSIONATE BUDDHA*
AND *THE WISDOM OF THE BUDDHIST MASTERS*

"In *Effortless Living*, Jason Gregory reminds us that a magic still dwells in our world despite the external forces, and psychological habits, that increasingly steer us toward cynicism. Gregory gives not only clear explanations of Taoism and reconciliations of it with Confucianism, but also guidelines for getting in touch with the Tao at the heart of all things. Furthermore, he makes clear why the root of world peace is the inner peace of the individual, which is why—socially and environmentally—this book is so deeply valuable. This is the best book on Taoism as a spiritual path since Alan Watts wrote *Tao: The Watercourse Way* nearly fifty years ago, and so I say, it's about time."

DANA SAWYER, PROFESSOR OF RELIGION AND PHILOSOPHY AT THE MAINE
COLLEGE OF ART AND AUTHOR OF *ALDOUS HUXLEY: A BIOGRAPHY*

"In this work the Tao is alive, expressing through itself, as itself! The words propel us through the labyrinth of mind to point us directly at the profound truths of our being, that mysterious Way which transcends the intellect and filters of the human mind. The book reverberates with the perennial truth that the great saints and sages of antiquity have taught. With clarity and insight we come to see the place of techniques and practices as well as their limitations. The dismantling of mind is palpable as we are pointed over and over again to the limits of the words themselves and a possibility of an opening, a dawning of that which we always already are but have forgotten."

DANIEL SCHMIDT, DOCUMENTARY FILMMAKER OF
INNER WORLDS, OUTER WORLDS AND *SAMADHI*

"In *Effortless Living*, Gregory portrays beautifully the ideas of hard-and-fast belief colliding with the natural harmony of true living with the flow of our natural state of being. This book also wonderfully explains how our need to control is more of an illusion that creates the very struggles that we see in our modern world; control interrupts the natural flow of life."

STEVEN L. HAIRFIELD, PhD, AUTHOR OF
A METAPHYSICAL INTERPRETATION OF THE BIBLE

EFFORTLESS LIVING

Wu-Wei and the Spontaneous
State of Natural Harmony

JASON GREGORY

Inner Traditions
Rochester, Vermont • Toronto, Canada

Inner Traditions
One Park Street
Rochester, Vermont 05767
www.InnerTraditions.com

SUSTAINABLE FORESTRY INITIATIVE
Certified Sourcing
www.sfiprogram.org
SFI-00854

Text stock is SFI certified

Library of Congress Cataloging-in-Publication Data

Names: Gregory, Jason, 1980– author.
Title: Effortless living : wu-wei and the spontaneous state of natural harmony /
 Jason Gregory.
Description: Rochester, Vermont : Inner Traditions, 2018. |
 Includes bibliographical references and index.
Identifiers: LCCN 2018000944 (print) | LCCN 2017026830 (e-book) |
 ISBN 9781620557136 (pbk.) | ISBN 9781620557143 (e-book)
Subjects: LCSH: Taoist philosophy.
Classification: LCC B162.7 (print) | LCC B162.7 .G74 2018 (e-book) |
 DDC 181/.114—dc23
LC record available at https://lccn.loc.gov/2018000944

Printed and bound in the United States by Lake Book Manufacturing, Inc.
The text stock is SFI certified. The Sustainable Forestry Initiative® program
promotes sustainable forest management.

10   9   8   7   6   5   4   3   2   1

Text design and layout by Priscilla Baker
This book was typeset in Garamond Premier Pro with Cinzel and Avant Garde
used as display typefaces

To send correspondence to the author of this book, mail a first-class letter to the
author c/o Inner Traditions • Bear & Company, One Park Street, Rochester, VT
05767, and we will forward the communication, or contact the author directly at
jasongregory.org.

Dedicated to the ancient Chinese master Lao-tzu.

May his wisdom continue to enlighten the world.

Contents

PART 1

THE ORIGIN OF THE
EFFORTLESS MIND IN THE EAST

PART 2

THE SCIENCE AND PRACTICE OF
AN EFFORTLESS MIND

PART 3

THE ART OF EFFORTLESS LIVING

Note on the Romanization of Chinese Words

There are two commonly known romanization systems for Chinese words. The older and more familiar one is known as the Wade-Giles, while the new standard and more precise one is the Pinyin romanization. For example, the Chinese word 道 in the Wade-Giles system is *Tao,* and this is the romanization that many people are familiar with. It is somewhat pleasing aesthetically, but its sound is not quite accurate. On the other hand, the Pinyin romanization of this word is *Dao.* Many are not familiar with this spelling, nor, may we say, is it as aesthetically pleasing, but its sound is more accurate. In this book I have blended both systems of romanization for Chinese and give the spelling of both when we are first introduced to a significant Chinese word in the text. The romanization I choose for each Chinese word is based on what I believe people are most familiar with and also what I feel is best aesthetically.

Shedding Skin to Liberate the Mind

Damo Mitchell

As a lifelong devotee of the Tao (道) only one thing has really ever held me back in my practice: a lack of trust. What is it that a true human should trust in?

We should give our trust to our unfolding path in life, which presents itself to us once we learn how to let go. This is both the simplest and most difficult of principles.

What stops a person from letting go and embracing trust in the unfoldment of the universe in their life is the interventions of the intellect. All those who walk the path of Tao will at some point or another realize that it is the machinations of their own minds that are preventing them from attaining the heightened states of consciousness alluded to by the ancient wisdom traditions. The nature of Tao is to flow and let life unfold in a harmonious manner. Those who can tap into this flow will be led toward a state of conscious elevation; those who cannot will generally be led down a path of trivial concerns.

This was the underlying ethos of the teachings of the ancient Chinese master Lao-tzu (老子), and for generations since it has been this deceptively difficult challenge that has lain at the heart of the Taoist tradition.

If we look at the majority of modern interpretations of Taoism, we see the hallmarks of a tradition that has sadly lost its way. Obscuring the original tenets are layer upon layer of useless trappings: ritual, hierarchy, worship, and other things generally associated with organized religion. Certainly the contemporary format of Taoism does not follow the teachings of its founders, nor does it serve to do anything but drag its adherents into a mire of trappings.

Having invested a great deal of my time and energy into a study of Taoism, I can see that my early years were concerned with learning as much as I could. I would study with any teacher I could find, spare no expense to travel to distant parts of Asia, and run myself ragged accumulating more and more information. The intellectual part of my mind thrived on my actions, but one day the realization dawned upon me that I was still no closer to really experiencing the Tao. I could perform no end of exercises, movements, and practices. I could quote classics and speak for hours on the theory of Taoism according to others, but I had no direct knowledge of what Tao meant. It was at this stage in my personal development that I understood that I needed to begin shedding. I needed to unclutter myself from the various trappings of Tao that I had accumulated, as it was these that were holding me back on my journey.

It is interesting for me to see how the majority of travelers within the internal arts go through a similar process. Those that move diligently enough along their path come to similar conclusions, so the process of unloading that which is unnecessary becomes the path itself. Those who never fully come to terms with the nature of Taoism unfortunately miss this important point and instead continue to accumulate.

As this uncluttering takes place, it begins an unfolding process within the mind so that the most sincere practitioners begin to realize the nature of *wu-wei* (無為). Here, within the (non)act of nondoing, lies the heart of the Taoist tradition. Through noninterference in the natural flow of the cosmos, spontaneous truth is realized from within. As the great Taoist teacher Wang Chong (王充) said: "The Way to Heaven is to take no action."

Within *Effortless Living* Jason Gregory eloquently explores the nature of Taoism and the concept of wu-wei from the position of somebody who has truly walked the path. This is a great relief to me, as I have grown tired of reading book after book written by pure Taoist theorists who butcher the tradition and in particular the nature of wu-wei through analysis from a position of pure intellect. It was like a breath of fresh air to spend time reading a text written by a true follower of the Way. As each chapter unfolds, you can see how Jason Gregory has been through the process of learning how to trust, let go, and manifest wu-wei through his very being. It is only when the majority of books on the nature of Tao are once again written by followers of the Way that Taoist literature will stop being so poor!

It also interested me greatly to see how Jason expertly brings the teachings of Taoism through into the modern age. An exploration of the nature of society and how it has developed in direct opposition to the way of Tao is by no means a mere modernism: a discomfort with societal structure has always been present within Taoism throughout history, but few writers seem to pick up on this. When I engage with the writings of Lao-tzu, Chuang-tzu (莊子), or indeed the vast majority of spiritual teachers around the world, I am confronted with radicals, misfits, and rebels. These are not prophets advocating the status quo; these are people who understood that stepping out of the structured nature of religion, society, and government was the only way to find some kind of personal liberation. What I learn from this is that only those who recognize the inherent sickness that pervades our societal structure will ever really be able to free themselves from the shackles of our societal paradigm. We are encouraged to live according to a narrative generated by a group of people who most certainly do not understand the concept of wu-wei, nor do they flow with the force of Tao. Rebellion is the natural inclination of many people who come to these conclusions, but in truth rebellion itself is against the flow of Taoism, because it too is a form of governance based within the acquired aspect of human mind. The real answer lies once again in the simplicity of wu-wei, the act of letting go and the trust that a new and spontaneous way of living will emerge.

Effortless Living is an important book, one that demands a place within anyone's mind, and especially any follower of the Way's library of resources. In putting it together Jason Gregory has undertaken a challenging task. One key reason that writing anything about Taoism is difficult is that the very tradition itself tells us right from early on in its key texts that it is practically impossible to discuss the nature of Taoism! It is a tradition that essentially transcends the limited language of words, and yet at the same time the medium of language is required if the tradition is to be passed on. This is a difficulty I have encountered when writing my own books. Often I am left scratching my head at the problem of putting into the written language a feeling or realization that comes from deep within the center of consciousness— an abstract sense of "knowing" that people have to reach themselves to truly connect with. Despite these difficulties and the experiential nature of the tradition, it is the language of words that points the way and sets a person's intention on the correct path. If I were to sit and consider how I would clearly and accurately put together a text describing the philosophical principle of wu-wei, I would certainly struggle, and yet with this book Jason Gregory has done an outstanding job of doing just that.

In conclusion, I would like to add that I truly believe it is important that any author or teacher within an internal tradition be a sincere adherent of the philosophy. If such a person does not embody the teachings in his own life, then he is simply adding to the watering-down of a timeless tradition as well as leading readers and students into the proverbial wilderness. As my role as head of an internal arts school has developed, I have found myself in many situations where I am mixing with other teachers and writers. The first thing I am curious about is the level of authenticity I find within these people. In many cases I am saddened to discover that they do not walk the path they are purporting to. Hypocrisy is an ugly human trait, and one that I have come to realize is rife throughout too many walks of life. In Chiang Mai, northern Thailand, I had the opportunity to spend time with Jason Gregory and his wife, Gayoung. Over the course of our conversations it was clear that Jason had explored the meaning and practices within many different systems, and that his journey has truly enabled the teachings of the Eastern traditions to guide his life and release his *xing* (性), his nature. By letting go and putting trust in the nature of wu-wei, Jason has reached a state of being untethered to the restricting state of the world. As such, he has achieved a liberation of spirit that makes him more than qualified to write such a book. I believe that in this book, Jason's study, as well as his ability to put his conclusions into writing, has created an instant classic within the Taoist tradition.

DAMO MITCHELL is a teacher of the internal arts of China and follows the classical threefold path of martial arts, medicine, and meditation. His teachings are based on the philosophy that Dao is to be found when these three areas of study come into harmony with one another. His studies began at the age of four years old and have developed full-time throughout his life to include in-depth cultivation within several traditional lineages. He runs the Lotus Nei

Gong International School of Daoist Arts, which has branches across Europe and America, as well as the Xian Tian College of Chinese Medicine, which focuses on both contemporary and classical therapeutic methods. He is the author of a number of books on the Daoist arts and continues to travel extensively and deepen his own studies between teaching events.

Acknowledgments

I started writing *Effortless Living* back in 2013 in a small apartment in Seoul, South Korea. Since then this book has been on a journey around the world for over three years, from Seoul to Chiang Mai in Thailand to Tiruvannamalai in India on to Pokhara in Nepal and then back to Chiang Mai. It has changed shape many times, including numerous title changes, a stack of edits and reedits, and many additions and subtractions all along the way. There are many people to thank for persisting with me in the unfoldment of this book.

First and foremost, I am forever grateful to my wife, Gayoung. You showed extreme patience and tender care during this extended writing process. When I would let this book rest for months on end you would motivate me to persevere with it and inspire me to continue to overcome the obstacles this book presented. You always said the right thing at the right time to curb my anxiety, leading to insightful guidance. I am beyond fortunate to live a life with someone who embraces the rollercoaster of uncertainty. Our trust in this crazy ride called our life is the trust we have in the love we share with each other. Let's see where this rollercoaster will flip us next.

Secondly, a big hug and humble gratitude to all of the wonderful people at Inner Traditions and Bear & Company. Words cannot describe what you've all done for my work going forward. I am especially thankful to my acquisition editor, Jon Graham. Jon, you steered me through the whole process. You pushed me all the way. You knew this book could be so much more. Back in 2013 when I thought the book was finished, you intuitively knew that I could do better. And this process happened many times because I was too anxious to finish the book without understanding its true potential, which included a massive revision. Without your book industry knowledge and all-around wisdom this book would have remained on my bookshelf. Thank you for giving it wings to fly.

Next I owe a debt of gratitude to my two editors for this book. First of all, a big thank you to my copyeditor, Richard Smoley, for meticulously going over each line to make the text sparkle with clarity. Secondly, heartfelt gratitude to my project editor, Meghan MacLean. You've been my project editor for my three previous books, and I'm always astounded by your skill and wisdom. But this time you really outdid yourself. For you to be able to focus and do your work with minimal fuss just before and after the birth of your child is a testament to the amazing individual you are.

Effortless Living was extremely fortunate to have a foreword written by Taoist teacher of traditional martial arts Damo Mitchell. It's no surprise that our paths have crossed considering our mutual love for the internal arts and the Eastern mind they came from. Some of my fondest memories are when you and your wife, Roni, visited Chiang Mai. I enjoyed gallivanting around northern Thailand with both of you. It's not common that two authors write a foreword for each other's books, but I'm proud to have written one for you and to have you provide one for *Effortless Living*.

Last but definitely not least, a humble bow to three of the great sages of the Warring States period of China: Lao-tzu, Confucius, and Chuang-tzu. All three were the inspiration behind this book.

Though their views may differ, and even though I may appear critical of Confucius in this book, we are truly blessed to have open access to all their wisdom. Now more than ever their wisdom is needed. *Effortless Living* hopes to carry their wisdom into the future.

The Effortless Mind

The experience of effortless mind is something we commonly attribute to athletes, artists, writers, poets, and philosophers. This state of consciousness is not bound by the limitations of the mind, but rather finds infinite expression and laserlike focus within the limited framework of our mental capacities and lives. We generally think of this mental state as *being in the zone.* We can sense this state when we watch a star athlete achieve the impossible or when a group of musicians improvise and feed off each other's energy to create a rhythmic synergy that nourishes our ears and inspires our hearts. Being in the zone is also the state of sustained concentration required to write a book, as I am doing right now. And yet there is an intrinsic paradox to being in the zone: in all crafts, to be effortlessly in the zone requires focused and sustained effort without any intention to achieve effortlessness within the mind. The effortless mind of the craftsman, then, is evoked by skillful effort *without* the intention of achieving that end. It is as though the craftsman and the craft are essentially one. Their effort is actually effortless because it is devoid of a person "doing" it; it is just happening spontaneously of itself in harmony with everything else.

The ability to focus the mind for a sustained period of time evokes the state of being in the zone, which allows us to achieve the impossible. This occurs because the conscious mind shuts down to allow the wisdom of the unconscious mind and body to take over. Muscle memory takes over, while the sense of "you" doing the task has been reduced.

According to cognitive science, the analytical conscious mind, the ego persona, what you refer to as "you," is located within the cerebral cortex, which covers the front of the frontal lobe of the brain. This part of the brain is known as the prefrontal cortex (PFC). It is a part of the brain that evolved later than many of the others in an effort to navigate through the increasing planetary obstacles we continually encountered. Cognitive science refers to the prefrontal cortex's analytical function as "cold cognition" or "System 2." Cold cognition is the cognitive control function of the mind, which gives us the ability to exert effort and discern between "this" and "that," and which formulates our opinions of "right" and "wrong" or "good" and "bad" based on our own personal experience. In our modern world the cold cognitive aspect of the mind is constantly overemployed from the beginning of life through education and then throughout working life, where it is thought that if we continue to force our effort continually, we will achieve our desired result. But as we all surely know, this is hardly ever achieved, because our focus is constantly distracted by the bombardment of external stimuli.

This analytical, active part of our mind in the prefrontal cortex is physiologically expensive if it is not supported by the more primal regions of the brain that we associate with the unconscious mind. The function of the unconscious regions of the brain is known in cognitive science as "hot cognition" or "System 1." Hot cognition is the function of our mind and body that is automatic, spontaneous, fast, effortless, mostly unconscious, and thought to be emotionally driven. Hot cognition is located within the earlier-developing primal regions of the brain and is associated with the unconscious. Its spontaneous and effortless function is what makes our head turn unconsciously when we see something beautiful in the environment, maybe a handsome man or ravishing woman, for example. And it can sometimes be a hindrance, as when we find ourselves unconsciously reaching for that piece of chocolate cake—a habit that arises from the way we evolved to seek sugar for momentary sustenance. On the one hand, hot cognition can produce all the miracles that spontaneously grow out of the mind and universe, and on the other hand it can lead us to being unhealthy (because there is an abundance of sugar that is constantly tempting us, for example). This is where the discernment of cold cognition is beneficial for our well-being.

The positive aspect of hot cognition is what drives those unconscious, spontaneous miracles achieved by many sports people; it is also what allows a musician to play her instrument without having to think about it. It is what allows artists, no matter whether they are painters, writers, musicians, gardeners, or athletes, to express the unconscious wisdom of the universe that lays dormant within our hot cognition. In all of these examples, the cold cognition within the prefrontal cortex that gave birth to the sense of "I," the personality, has shut down to allow the effortless flow of the universe to come to life. As a result, none of these creative types have to "think" to achieve the miraculous, and this is the effortless hallmark of being in the zone.

When we shut down our analytical, thinking mind, we achieve greatness. In India this is known as *grace,* and in ancient Asian thought it was understood that this grace comes about because of the ability to see that everything is done when left undone. Yet people were perplexed as to how a state of effortlessness within the mind can be attained with effort. Effortlessness, of course, implies no effort. As the American professor of Asian studies at the University of British Columbia Edward Slingerland has asked, how do we try not to try? In the ancient East most people were not craftsmen, and still are not, so they began to ask how they could attain the effortless, embodied skill of the craftsman as their everyday state of consciousness. People also wondered if being in the zone is beneficial, or even possible, in our ordinary lives.

In the ancient East wise people observed the mind of the craftsmen. They studied their ability to shut down their cold cognitive prefrontal cortex, so it appeared that their effort actually required no effort, as if their minds were at one with the universe's unfoldment. Craftsmen's work doesn't look like work; rather it looks as if their mind and body have been attuned to the rhythm and dance of an invisible realm that brings a real joy to their lives and at the same time inspires others.

Craftsmen have this ability to be one with their craft without the sense of a person "doing" it. This is what interested the wise of the ancient East. As a result, the documented birth of martial arts was based on the effortless mind of the craftsman. The martial artist focused on trying to cultivate an effortless mind, where being in the zone is one's ordinary state of mind *all* the time. The first traces of spiritually oriented martial arts, and their focus on health, longevity, and physical immortality, can be attributed to the philosophy of Yang Zhu (440–360 BCE: Wade-Giles, *Yang Chu;* Pinyin, *Yang Zhu*), who is credited with "the discovery of the body." His philosophy is known as Yangism. There is speculation that the oldest forms of martial arts in China go back to the Xia dynasty more than four thousand years ago, but there is not much evidence to support this claim, and it is suspected that these forms of martial arts were only combat oriented.

Nevertheless, the foundation of spiritually oriented Asian martial arts in its original form lay in trying to cultivate an effortless mind all the time. This is still the primary focus of spiritually oriented martial arts today: being in the zone is thought of as a state of consciousness we can be in constantly. But the problem for Yang Zhu, and for many martial artists, was that excessive effort was still required to get even close to the effortless state of consciousness. The sense of someone "doing" martial arts was still there, which essentially eclipses the main objective of the craft, which is to transform our character.

It is this sense of "I," the acquired personality, that is the primary focus in the East, because our true nature and reality can only be experienced when the "I" has vanished. The effortless mind of being in the zone is not something we can actively seek to attain, because this requires effort. Being in the zone is an art that is evoked by essentially doing nothing to attain it. From this perspective, even effort is cleansed of trying and striving, because the sense of "I" is not there. This art and wisdom goes back further than the original martial artists and craftsmen. This book focuses on revealing the origins and history of the effortless mind, as well as on how to apply this art and science to our lives. I will go back to the basis of zone thinking in order to reveal an art of being in the effortless mind all the time, as my book is an attempt to explain that the zone we usually only experience briefly is actually our true natural mind. This wisdom goes back to an ancient sage of the East and a classical text attributed to him over two thousand five hundred years ago.

THE HEART OF LIFE

Though the spiritual texts and literature of all religions and wisdom traditions may be vast, many appear to skirt around the essential teaching that masters lived and avoid saying how we can apply their teachings to our lives. This is especially true in the case of that ancient master of China Lao-tzu (Wade-Giles, *Lao-tzu;* Pinyin, *Laozi*). From the time at which it is assumed that Lao-tzu lived (the sixth century BCE) until the present day, we know of only a few rare beings who have lived and revealed the mysterious depth of his teachings. One of them was the great sage Chuang-tzu (369–286 BCE: Wade-Giles *Chuang-tzu;* Pinyin *Zhuangzi*). Many spiritual seekers, martial artists, and teachers are fixated on "eating the menu"—talking about or dancing around the main meal instead of tasting it; that is, not going directly to the heart of things. But going to the heart of things was the primary focus of Chuang-tzu. And this heart of things, according to him, is the mysterious "Tao of the Absolute," which is centered on aligning to the source and substance of this ever-changing universe, rather than the "Tao of things," which is focused on the temporary fluctuations of change that we usually seek to shape according to our own interests.

The *Tao* (道: Wade-Giles *Tao,* Pinyin *Dao*) of the Absolute is analogous to the Hindu *Brahman* and the Buddhist *Tathata,* and to the original concept of God in the monotheistic religions. Yet neither Lao-tzu nor Chuang-tzu is saying that the Tao cannot be known through the Tao of things. On the contrary, they both understood that the eternal presence of Tao courses through the veins of the entire phenomenal world, producing a metaphysical path that gives us a sense of guidance and order in relation to the universe within our ordinary lives. But they are attempting to explain that we become attracted only to the movement of energy within life, rather than to the source of our energy, which is the indescribable stillness at the heart of the human being and the universe. As a result, we have developed numerous methods of practice to explore this movement of energy through our bodies, such as the Chinese arts of qigong and t'ai chi, the Indian practice of hatha yoga, and the modern movement culture spreading across the globe. The problem with practical movement methods such as these is they can delay our quest for a liberated mind (enlightenment) if the practice becomes a habitual crutch.

A movement method becomes a habitual crutch when it is not backed up and supported by time spent in stillness. No real transformation of mind happens without regularly stilling the mind. This is evident with martial artists, hatha yogis, and movement practitioners who incorrectly believe that they have control of the mind because they have control of their bodies. But we discover that, although they have good control of their bodies, their minds still run amok and have not essentially transformed. The essential principle of martial arts, hatha yoga, and any movement method is that the practice is supposed to transform our character into being more humble and respectful, which reorients our focus to within ourselves, thus cleansing us of our wrong perception of self, others, and the world. The point of these practices is to be conscious of the inner world and reach the spiritual sphere. Without the exploration of stillness, the Tao of the Absolute, the spiritual sphere becomes a mirage, because practitioners become intoxicated with the outer world of materiality and with the feats they can achieve physically. And yet this perception is in stark contrast to the wisdom of Lao-tzu, on which the philosophy of martial arts and numerous movement methods are built.

Nowhere within the beautiful verses of Lao-tzu's classic text the *Tao Te Ching* does he suggest that liberation is a bodily adventure of practice and discipline instead of a psychological freedom. Actually Lao-tzu does not teach any physical or mental exercise in the very small fragments of text he left behind. That only began with Yang Zhu's interpretation of Lao-tzu's philosophy.

The mysterious nature of Lao-tzu's lucid wisdom is the very reason why a multitude of interpretations of the inner meaning have surfaced. In fact, this is the genius of Lao-tzu's philosophy, because the *Tao Te Ching* has no definite interpretation. This is the reason why the Tao referred to in the text could be molded to suit martial arts, other spiritual practices, or even business and war.

Though it may appear that I am criticizing martial artists, hatha yogis, movement practitioners, and spiritual practices somewhat, I am not; to get to the heart of things we need to discuss the things that have developed around Lao-tzu's wisdom since his time. In fact, I am always actively engaged in various forms of spiritual cultivation in my daily life, and I am also an avid admirer of those who have mastered this art of cultivation, especially martial artists, hatha yogis, and movement practitioners. But what I am trying to explain, in a sense, is a mirror of Lao-tzu's understanding, which is that any method of martial or spiritual practice is a means rather than an end. This end, which is eclipsed by our spiritual practice, is the psychological liberation of enlightenment. In *Zen and the Psychology of Transformation,* French psychotherapist Hubert Benoit explains this confusion between our attempts toward realization (enlightenment; *satori* in Japanese, *moksha* in Sanskrit) and the actuality of the experience:

> The error which consists in considering realisation as the success of a training is epitomised in the adhesion given by so many men to systematic methods: the conception of this or that "ideal," yogas of one kind or another, "moral systems" proclaiming that such automatisms should be installed and such others eliminated, in short any kind of discipline to which one attributes an intrinsic efficacity for realisation. *The error is not in doing and putting to the test what these methods require, the error does not consist in following these methods; it consists in believing that these methods can result by themselves in satori as roads issue at the end of a journey.*

But this advice is hard to understand in the right way. If I see in it a condemnation of training I am mistaken, for this condemnation does not free me from evaluation; it only results in an inversion of training. In this false understanding I would train myself to train myself no longer, which would change nothing; I would be believing, without escaping from my error, in the efficacity for realisation of a counter-training which would still be a training. Zen tells us not to lay a finger on life: "Leave things as they may be." It is not for me to modify directly my habits of training myself. It is only indirectly that I can obtain the disappearance of these habits, by means of my understanding, ever more profound, that these attempts at training, which I continue to make, have in themselves no efficacity for realisation. It is a question, in short, of obtaining the devalorisation of these compensations which are my attempts at training; and this implies the defeat of the attempts and the correct interpretation of this defeat. I am not obliged to concern myself with the defeat; that will flow from the very nature of things; but I am concerned with the correct interpretation of this defeat. If I believe in the intrinsic efficacity of a discipline, I attribute its failure to all kinds of things but not to the discipline itself; so that it does not devalorise itself. If, on the contrary, I have understood the intrinsic inefficacity of the discipline, while not by any means forbidding myself to practice it if I feel the need to do so, a profound lassitude will develop little by little in me which will detach me from this discipline in a real *transcendence*.

Satori, as we know, is not the crowning of an ultimate success but of an ultimate defeat. The consciousness of always having been free appears in us when we have exhausted all the attempts, all the training, that we believe may be capable of liberating us. If the disciplines could not be paths resulting in satori, that does not mean that they may not be paths to be followed; they are paths leading to blind-alleys, all leading to a unique and ultimate blind-alley; but they are to be followed just because satori cannot be obtained unless we have come up against the end of this last blind alley. They are to be followed with the theoretical understanding that they lead nowhere, so that experience may transform this theoretical understanding into total understanding, into this clear vision which is the arrival in the blind-alley and which lays us open to satori.[1]

We are more attracted to the practice of spiritual cultivation than to what the practice is supposed to reveal. We are not willing to accept the ultimate defeat humbly, as Benoit puts it. As a result, we continue to exhibit gross spiritual pride toward our so-called attainments. This attitude can be directed toward practice of any kind. This psychological tendency is known as eating the menu. In *Effortless Living* I am not interested in discussing the contents of the menu with you, even though we may trace over them to better understand the meal. This book is concerned with taking you beyond the menu to finally taste the ineffable mystery of Lao-tzu's sublime dinner.

THE FUNDAMENTAL CHINESE PHILOSOPHY OF WU-WEI

In order to taste the delicious meal Lao-tzu provided for humanity, we need to understand the core tenet of almost all Chinese philosophical systems. This foundational pillar of Chinese philosophy is found within the classics of Eastern thought, notably the *Tao Te Ching*, the *Analects* of Confucius, the *Chuang-tzu*, attributed to Chuang-tzu, and even the Indian text the *Bhagavad Gita*.

The core pillar of these classics, in China especially, is believed to originate from Lao-tzu, and it is his essential teaching that is veiled within the mystery of the Chinese word *wu-wei* (無為: Wade-Giles *wu-wei*, Pinyin *wu-wei*) (see figure I.1), which is the core of Chinese philosophy and a predominant principle in Eastern thought. This word is shrouded in misinterpretation. The main confusion arises from the Confucian translation of *wei-wu-wei*, which literally means "doing nondoing." This interpretation is built on Confucius's philosophy of trying to install the eternal Tao and its virtue into our character as if it were some external agency. This is the completely opposite perspective to Lao-tzu's teaching of naturalness. Translated into English, *wu-wei* means "nondoing," "nonaction," or "effortless action." These translations are literally correct and lead us to the intuitive and ultimate psychological experience of wu-wei. This effortless psychological experience means "not forcing" or "allowing," a state of "intelligent spontaneity." The Trappist monk and author Thomas Merton describes wu-wei transparently in his book *The Way of Chuang Tzu*:

Figure I.1. Wu-wei—nondoing / not forcing / effortless action
By Dao Stew

The true character of wu wei is not mere inactivity but *perfect action*—because it is act without activity. In other words, it is action not carried out independently of Heaven and earth and in conflict with the dynamism of the whole, but in perfect harmony with the whole. It is not mere passivity, but it is action that seems both effortless and spontaneous because performed "rightly," in perfect accordance with our nature and with our place in the scheme of things. It is completely free because there is in it no force and no violence. It is not "conditioned" or "limited" by our own individual needs and desires, or even by our own theories and ideas.[2]

In alignment with Thomas Merton's description of wu-wei is the ancient Indian story of Krishna and Arjuna in the *Bhagavad Gita*. The similarity comes from the Sanskrit *nishkam karma,* which means to remain active but be inwardly effortless, without any need of being rewarded for the fruits of labor. Krishna wants Arjuna to be so effortless that his actions are completely selfless and the sense of "I" has dissolved. The *Bhagavad Gita* states this in two key verses:

> *To action alone hast thou a right and never at all to its fruits;*
> *let not the fruits of action be thy motive; neither let there be in*
> *thee any attachment to inaction.*

Fixed in yoga, do thy work, O Winner of wealth (Arjuna),
abandoning attachment, with an even mind in success and
failure, for evenness of mind is called yoga.[3]

In the cosmic sphere of energy, wu-wei is the feminine (passive/receptive/Earth) principle of the universe. Psychologically within a human, it is the attribute of humility, which is more of an ontological or cosmic humility than the unctuousness of Uriah Heep in Charles Dickens's novel *David Copperfield*. The wu-wei at the core of Lao-tzu's philosophy is not something we can understand by intellectual discourse or attain by rigorous practice. On the contrary, the depth of wu-wei is only revealed to us when we are humble enough to let go of controlling our lives and instead live by its spontaneous principle. When we do not force or try to control life, wu-wei is experienced within our consciousness. It is hidden within the depth of our psyche as the formless Way of Tao beyond conventional thought and definite interpretation. Wu-wei is not something we can categorically explain or point to as an object of knowledge. Wu-wei is the truth that can be known through experience but cannot be given a form to appease the intellect.

THE PARADOX OF LANGUAGE

Wu-wei is the eternal aphorism of Lao-tzu and of Taoism and the martial-arts culture that was established after his life. This aphorism is not limited to intellectual knowledge, because it always reflects different aspects of yourself back to you according to your stage of conscious growth. To try and teach the experience of or interpret wu-wei is to lose sight of its depth. And yet here I am, dedicating a whole book to its mystery and the ability to apply it to our lives. In the same fashion, Lao-tzu explains within the first lines of the *Tao Te Ching* that to try and interpret or give meaning to the Tao is to lose grasp of the Tao, but paradoxically he goes on to write eighty-one chapters. The first lines of the *Tao Te Ching* state:

> *The tao that can be told*
> *is not the eternal Tao.*
> *The name that can be named*
> *is not the eternal Name.*[4]

This form of paradox is a necessary tool in many spiritual teachings and traditions, especially those of the East. The use of language necessitates the paradox because it is paradoxical by nature. With language, for example, something either "is" or "isn't." We all know too well that there are always two sides to every argument or opinion. Language then becomes a device for explaining the field of duality only. It is a tool for partiality, which results in ignorance of nonpartiality. Cognitive science has revealed that language cannot have the same interpretation universally among all people, as Western thinkers originally believed. What one word meant to Lao-tzu is totally different to the way you and I may understand it.

Common misconceptions are built around language, especially among those who are spiritually inclined. The way people associate their understanding with certain words, such as consciousness, mind, awareness, perception, ego, self, truth, and God, all cause much confusion, because each word has the ability to change its meaning in correspondence to the growth of the individual. This confusion occurs even among people of the same language. On top of this, there is an immense amount of misinterpretation that is lost in translation from one language to another. In any event, language itself, no matter what dialect, is an inadequate tool for describing the nature of the universe.

Lao-tzu describes the limitations of language best in the first lines of the *Tao Te Ching*, as we see from the passage above. Investigating language, we discover that it consists of ideas, sounds, thoughts, and words, which are structured building blocks contained within reality and are subject to its processes. Language cannot fully describe all of reality, because language is a part of that reality. Paradoxically, the microcosmic part of a human being contains the whole universe, but it is language that conceals our innate connection to, and identity with, the universe. A journey into the paradoxical nature of language can reveal this relationship between the macrocosmic universe and the microcosmic human being.

Exploring both sides of the coin of life has its benefits. We discover, as a result, the nonpartial perspective that Chuang-tzu demonstrated best. Discovering the paradoxical nature within our language and psyche reveals another "Way." This is the doctrine of the *Middle Way* practiced in Buddhism, where opposites are thought to be mutual rather than in opposition. Our overstimulated intellect, which is constantly discerning between "this" and "that," eclipses this mysterious Way with many mental sheaths. Contradiction in thought and language and the emergence of the Middle Way fly in the face of conventional logic. This perspective was embraced in ancient China with the birth of dialecticism because the Chinese use paradox, especially in language, to understand life. American psychologist Richard Nisbett articulates the essence of the paradoxical Middle Way of language and thought in his book *The Geography of Thought:*

The Chinese dialectic instead uses contradiction to understand relations among objects or events, to transcend or integrate apparent oppositions, or even to embrace clashing but instructive viewpoints. In the Chinese intellectual tradition there is no necessary incompatibility between the belief that A is the case and the belief that not-A is the case. On the contrary, in the spirit of the Tao or yin-yang principle, A can actually imply that not-A is also the case, or at any rate soon will be the case. Dialectical thought is in some ways the opposite of logical thought. It seeks not to decontextualize but to see things in their appropriate contexts: Events do not occur in isolation from other events, but are always embedded in a meaningful whole in which the elements are constantly changing and rearranging themselves. To think about an object or event in isolation and apply abstract rules to it is to invite extreme and mistaken conclusions. It is the Middle Way that is the goal of reasoning.[5]

Psychologically, the intellect is the masculine principle of the universe, or in Chinese *yang* (陽: Wade-Giles *yang*, Pinyin *yang*), and its habitual tendency is geared toward force and control. On the other end of the spectrum, the feminine principle of the universe, or in Chinese *yin* (陰: Wade-Giles *yin*, Pinyin *yin*), is the intuition and heart of our existence, which perceives reality as it *is* rather than what we would like it to be according to our intellect and imagination. The characteristic of the feminine yin principle is analogous to space, because space is soft, receptive, and formless, and its natural essence lies in the humility of not forcing, of allowing and receptiveness, which are all attributes of the mysterious wu-wei.

Our conditioned tendency toward hyperintellectualism veils and obscures the truth discovered beneath its parameters. This is not to say that the intellect is a problem that we need to eradicate. On the contrary, it is an important part of our existence, but the problem is that we have overemphasized the intellect. This keeps us in memories of the past and in the imagination or projection of the future, while never being in the *reality* of the present moment.

Our suffering as a species comes from the incorrect perception of living in the past through our attachment to memories that then shape our future. The phantoms of past and future are only of use to the intellect, because it gives individuals the idea that they are in control of their lives. Yet, as an individual grows, he begins to understand that no matter how grandiose his attempts at control, life always has a way of changing those plans. And in doing so, life also destroys the individual's imagined ability to control the future outcome. This mentality of forcing ourselves upon life is the socially accepted practice of modern civilization. An individual's attempt to control life according to her own beliefs, and as a result to force this perspective upon others, is the beginning of tyranny. Lao-tzu's essential teaching of wu-wei, on the other hand, illustrates the futility of our attempts to control life. He emphasizes that it is only when you give up forcing or controlling anything that you begin to get the kind of control you always wanted, but never knew existed.

The experience of wu-wei unlocks this mystery when our life comes into accord with not forcing ourselves upon any aspect of life. Our consciousness becomes transparent and reflective, like a still body of water, when we experience the depth of wu-wei, and even if this water is disturbed by insurmountable waves, they often settle quite quickly, because we move with the current instead of opposing it.

Understanding and following the mystery of wu-wei does not mean that you lose your intellectual faculties. Instead, your intellectual life and the apparent use of force begin to be refined into a changeful openness toward life. Actually our intellectual life begins to thrive when we relinquish the habit of force. The use of force begins to lose its velocity when the intellect softens and marinates in the effortless heart of wu-wei. But we never fully discard the use of intellect, which brings us back to the paradox of Lao-tzu's wisdom. The reason he continues to write eighty-one chapters of the *Tao Te Ching* after explaining within the first few lines that the mystery of the Tao cannot be intellectually understood is that intellect and force are the apparatus of language. They are only a cloak to dress the real world of no force, the effortless wu-wei. The art of wu-wei is shining through the intellectual landscape of words within Lao-tzu's *Tao Te Ching*. His words veil the truth, yet the words are necessary symbols to transform your consciousness from ignorance into the field of that unspeakable reality which Lao-tzu called Tao.

Effortless Living is an audacious attempt to explain Lao-tzu's essential wisdom for the benefit of the modern world. But be mindful that this book is not going to give you a categorical explanation of what the experience of wu-wei *is*. That onus and responsibility are yours. They are determined by how much you want a liberated mind. What *Effortless Living* will attempt to explain is the inner meaning of wu-wei and the art of living it. It is entirely up to you to digest and assimilate *Effortless Living* so that Lao-tzu's essential wisdom is brought to life through your own experience. The essential teaching of wu-wei can only be known if the individual is sincere in surrendering control and, as a result, giving his life over to something much bigger than himself.

Tao is *That* which is bigger than our personal lives. Its depth of understanding is vast. Wu-wei is the fragrance of Tao. It is the spiritual attitude that is expressed and lived by many adepts, gurus, masters, saints, sages, shamans, and yogis. When we discover the flow of Tao moving within our own lives, as a sage does, we begin to be receptive to where our experience in life is leading us. We cease clinging to the experiences of the past and instead become rejuvenated in the present. The future becomes nothing more than a mirage, as the pure transparency and reflectivity of our consciousness begins to be absorbed in the feminine womb of the Tao.

When you don't force yourself upon life, you discover that you *are* life. All our vain attempts to control life result from the way we are raised, because our culture and society influence us to believe that we do not belong to the world. We are taught to feel like aliens in this world, like in a great cosmic joke with no punch line. We are raised to believe that we exist in a hostile universe, so we ought to fear one another and never trust anyone. This ideology is bringing the human race to its knees. At the rate of speed that we are polarizing ourselves, it is hard to imagine there will be any remnants of higher, conscious life on this planet a thousand years from now. Our lack of trust is destroying our civilization and also causing a huge dent in the animal, plant, and mineral kingdoms.

This type of neurosis has gotten to the point that on an individual level we do not even trust our own psychological states. We do not act authentically, and we confuse our identity with our social identity. In being mere shadows of who we are, we cause violence toward others, condemn anyone who opposes our opinion, and hypnotically hurt those we love. All of this is done in the name of force and control. Social and cultural norms teach us this dichotomy. To act or function any other way is, from the point of view of the status quo, absurd.

Government, organized religion, society, and culture mark the physical advent of the trust that is lacking within the individual. If individuals lose their natural essence of trust, then some form of external tyranny in the guise of a trustworthy parental figure will take its place. Individuals fail to trust themselves, and this is why a lot people ignorantly trust their government without question. In giving our power away to government, the individual begins to depend on the government as a parent, rather than seeing it in its original position— as a servant to the individual. Our lack of responsibility implies our lack of trust in ourselves.

Government is a phantom into which we invest too much energy. Individuals who sincerely trust themselves and others threaten the established order of culture, society, organized religion, and government. This threat could only become a reality if the truth of Tao is regained and a trust in life is realized. Wu-wei is the Taoist principle of trust. The trust of wu-wei threatens any governmental, social, religious, and cultural landscape. We align with our innate trust when we are not forcing and instead allow life to take place. This capacity to align with your innate trust brings you back in harmony with the entire unfolding of the cosmos. To go with the grain or with a stream, one is not bound to the past, nor does one yearn for the future.

This grain or stream conforms to a cosmic organic pattern, which is the order of how the universe functions. The organic pattern is known as *li* (理: Wade-Giles *li,* Pinyin *li*) in Chinese. If we look into the grain of wood, the markings of a tortoise shell, the skin of an elephant, the spiral pattern of a sunflower, our own palms, and so on, we discover the organic pattern of li, which in some cases is mathematically fixed to the Golden Ratio of the Fibonacci sequence discovered by the thirteenth-century Italian mathematician Leonardo Fibonacci. Tao is what courses through the pattern of li, and this fundamental process beautifies our world. Before his untimely death in 1973, the British philosopher Alan Watts explained li in his last book *Tao: The Watercourse Way:*

> The Chinese call this kind of beauty the following of li, an ideogram which referred originally to the grain in jade and wood, and which [Joseph] Needham translates as "organic pattern," although it is more generally understood as the "reason" or "principle" of things. Li is the pattern of behavior which comes about when one is in accord with the Tao, the watercourse of nature. The patterns of moving air are of the same character, and so the Chinese idea of elegance is expressed as *feng-liu,* the following of wind.[6]

Coming into accord with li means we are coming into accord with that mysteriously eternal Tao. We cannot unite with the source of Tao unless we have given our life over to the nondoing, nonforcing, and nonreactive realm of wu-wei. Lao-tzu's essential wisdom is nothing more than that of an individual who can follow the effortless grace of wu-wei within her mind. Everything else that has developed around Lao-tzu's essential wisdom is a way either to get to the understanding of wu-wei or to delay our enlightenment through habitual crutches that take the form of spiritual exercises and practices. From the perspective of the ancient masters Lao-tzu and Chuang-tzu, enlightenment can only be realized in the ability to live wu-wei.

Almost all facets of what is perceived as Taoism since the time of Lao-tzu have turned this meditative, experiential way into a structure of control, hence *not* wu-wei. Within part 1 of *Effortless Living,* I will give a critical analysis of the difference between the religion of Taoism, which was built around the teachings of Lao-tzu with his essential wisdom of wu-wei and which gave birth to the martial and spiritual sphere of Chinese thought, and Confucian thinking. In part 2, I will explain the science of bringing the virtue of an effortless mind to society and culture, which could transform our concept of government into something much greater. We will also explore the power we possess from gaining the ability to trust and live spontaneously, which are the core components for the practice of being in the zone. In part 3 it all comes together to provide us the depth to live the art of an effortless mind. *Effortless Living* will reveal that if we choose to follow this humble path paved before us by Lao-tzu, then we will gain the individual liberation that many people believe comes from the liberation of society. This individual liberation, according to Lao-tzu, is what secretly transforms and liberates the world. The practice of wu-wei is the vehicle we use to realize our innate freedom. This book may give us a chance to rediscover the art of effortless living, wu-wei.

PART 1

The Origin of the Effortless Mind in the East

1

The Way of Nature Is No Ideology or Theology

When the word *Taoism* is uttered, many people identify it with a religion. But was Lao-tzu teaching and setting up an organized religion? Similarly we could ask whether the intent of Jesus of Nazareth was to create Christianity or whether Siddhartha Gautama's intent was to create Buddhism. Throughout history we discover that religions are often formed many years after the focal point of a religion's doctrine, in the form of an enlightened sage, has died. The intent of all legendary sages is to liberate the individual from the shackles of separation and suffering.

The legends of Lao-tzu, Krishna, Rama, Gautama the Buddha, and Jesus of Nazareth align with each other through an ineffable mystery that is veiled within their stories. None of these sages mandated that a religion should be organized around a group of precepts. On the contrary, they had no interest in setting up dogmas based around their teachings, because the essence of their teachings is a formless mystery. We invariably create dogmas when we do not understand the depth of the knowledge we are trying to comprehend. As a result, we cloak such knowledge by giving it a name and form in order to try and somehow make sense of it. This appears to be a typical psychological trait that shelters us from the real essence of what we are trying to know.

In many cases, words such as *Tao, Brahman, Tathata, Allah, Akasha, God,* and so on, conjure up an air of confusion for the average individual because the bulk of humanity do not observe or center themselves upon the source of the world, which is within oneself. Most people are focused on the outside world and are subject to the hypnotic belief that this is where the world exists. As a result, when they hear a word such as *God,* they cannot conceive of "what" it is. They mold its meaning to the world they think they know, which is the world of form and pleasure. Hypnotically, we give anthropomorphic form to that mystery. This somehow appeases our intellect, and we think we have figured out that God is some sort of Being above us, lording it over everything. Religious wars are waged tirelessly from this absurd monarchical view of God. This tyrannical view is also found in Taoism as a religious notion, which would bring a confused look to the face of Lao-tzu.

THE TAO OF THE OLD MASTER

Out of all the spiritual paths lived by the legendary sages, Taoism would be the least likely to have become a religion. Never did Lao-tzu explain a doctrine that one could follow. He knew that this would wind up in intellectual conjecture. The Taoism of Lao-tzu was about the Way, the Tao, which is something we experience when we are more attentive to our inner and outer worlds. The Tao can be followed and experientially known when we have surrendered our controlled, conditioned identity over to the effortless realm of spontaneity and trust, wu-wei. This effortless realm is why the Tao is usually referred to as "the way of nature," because when we follow the Way, we can experience the same spontaneity of nature within our own experience; as a result, we trust our path through life. The discovery of this spontaneity in life allows us to sink deeply into the awareness that we *are* nature and not separate from any aspect of it. This revelation of oneness with nature reveals a close relationship between the shamanic traditions of antiquity and the wisdom of Lao-tzu, minus the rites and rituals. In the essential teaching of Lao-tzu we discover small traces of some connection to the ancient shamanic traditions of China going way back into the Shang dynasty (1600–1046 BCE).

But in no way could there be any connection to shamanic practices, ancestral worship, sacrifice, rites, and rituals, because knowing and following the Tao according to Lao-tzu has nothing to do with outward gestures, no matter how dazzling to the eye. All forms of practice and ritual are controlling aspects of the intellect and its repetitive modes rather than natural spontaneity. We could say, however, that in ancient times they were performed because they expressed the concealed mystical truth of Tao. Lao-tzu was not against such activities, but he did become concerned when people viewed them as a form of liberation.

Both the great sages Lao-tzu and Chuang-tzu explained that the real Way of Tao is beyond the outward form. Instead of being concerned with the temporality of such things as rituals, we can directly access the depth of our being through the feminine quality of wu-wei. Yet the teachings of Lao-tzu have been discarded in favor of the shamanic practices, ancestral worship, sacrifice, rites, and rituals that have developed and been embraced by the world since his time. All of this came about from the misinterpretation of Lao-tzu's teachings by the social moralist Confucius and others down the line of history.

CONFUCIAN MORALITY AND THE PHILOSOPHY OF *JU*

Confucianism is still the predominant philosophy of East Asia. Aspects of Confucianism are not only found in China but are embedded in many different ideologies around the world. Confucianism is the moral and ethical outgrowth from the Taoist philosophy of Lao-tzu. We could only hazard a guess about whether Lao-tzu and Confucius knew each other.

When we study the mind of Confucius, we discover a man who understood the Taoist Way well and was a key contributor to the classic Taoist oracle the *I Ching*. But when we dissect the moral virtue of Confucius's superior man, we discover that his interpretation of Lao-tzu's wisdom may have only reached an intellectual level. This is because his primary focus was not on the liberation of the individual but on an enlightened society. I am not saying here that an enlightened society is impossible. But it needs to be clear that the foundation of a society comes from what is within the minds of the individuals who live in it. Hence Lao-tzu's insight is that the enlightenment of the individual takes us a step closer to the total liberation of humankind.

This should make complete sense to anybody. Yet we have devised a whole social system of thought based on the concept that it is not the individual pieces that make up the whole, but rather it is the whole that controls the pieces. Surely you can recognize this idiosyncratic view of life within yourself. The German philosopher Friedrich Nietzsche once said in regard to morality within society, "Morality— the idiosyncrasy of decadents, with the ulterior motive of revenging themselves on life—successfully."[1]

This concept has led to the formation of institutional power, which wields its influence over the individual through government, religion, the economy, academia, and other institutions. Confucius's interpretation of Lao-tzu's wisdom contributed heavily to this confused view of reality. Confucianism was not an enhancement of the Taoist Way. On the contrary, it deformed its wisdom into a vehicle that would only suit the morally and ethically "noble" of society. The Confucian way is to try and transform the individual according to the moral codes and ethics of ju (儒: Wade-Giles *ju*, Pinyin *ru*) philosophy.

Ju philosophy is the heart of Confucius's teachings and the framework of Confucianism. It is constructed around four basic virtues (see figure 1.1). The first of these basic virtues is known in Chinese as *jen* (仁: Wade-Giles *jen*, Pinyin *ren*), which is translated in English as "human-heartedness." This human-heartedness is the compassion and devotional love we have deep down for one another. It is the ability to identify with the suffering and joy of others as if they were our own.

The second virtue is called *yi* (義: Wade-Giles *I*, Pinyin *yi*) in Chinese, which is the sense of justice, responsibility, duty, and obligations to others. We need to be mindful that both jen and yi are disinterested states: the superior man does not do anything that will please or profit himself, because jen and yi emanate from an unconditional moral imperative.

The third virtue is the Confucian concept of *li* (禮: Wade-Giles *li*, Pinyin *li*). But this principle is somewhat different from the Taoist li (理), which we have briefly mentioned in the introduction and will discuss at length within this book. Li in the Confucian ju philosophy is the acting out of love and veneration for those relationships that make up the identity of our life—for example, family, one's people, and also heaven and earth. Li in this case is the liturgical contemplation of the religious and metaphysical structure of an individual. In the li of ju philosophy, an individual is grateful to take his place in the social and cosmic order of life.

The fourth and final virtue is *chih* (智: Wade-Giles *chih*, Pinyin *zhi*), which means *wisdom* in Chinese. Chih combines the three other virtues into a religious maturity whereby one follows a spontaneous inner obe-

Figure 1.1. The four basic virtues of ju philosophy
By Dao Stew

dience toward heaven, rather than being moved by external influences.

Though ju philosophy may sound admirable compared to our modern code of conduct, it is still an artificial construct attempting to make the individual conform to a set of rules and a system of behavior. This fosters social unrest, because the individual loses her naturalness. The Confucian philosophy of ju still dictates a set of standard laws to the individual. As a result it is fundamentally flawed, because it implies that we do not belong to this world, and instead need a doctrine to live by.

LAO-TZU'S NATURAL INDIVIDUAL VERSUS CONFUCIUS'S SOCIAL ETHICS

The Taoism of Lao-tzu emphasizes that if we do not let individuals grow as nature intended, they will lose their naturalness and be drawn into the world of animal drives, desires, attachments, and ultimately suffering. This difference in the depth of understanding between Lao-tzu and Confucius is articulated in an imaginary dialogue created by Chuang-tzu:

"Tell me," said Lao-tzu, "in what consist charity and duty to one's neighbour?"

"They consist," answered Confucius, "in a capacity for rejoicing in all things; in universal love, without the element of self. These are the characteristics of charity and duty to one's neighbour."

"What stuff!" cried Lao-tzu. "Does not universal love contradict itself? Is not your elimination of self a positive manifestation of self? Sir, if you would cause the empire not to lose its source of nourishment—there is the universe, its regularity is unceasing; there are the sun and moon, their brightness is unceasing; there are the stars, their groupings never change; there are the birds and beasts, they flock together without varying; there are the trees and shrubs, they grow upwards without exception. Be like these: follow Tao, and you will be perfect. Why then these vain struggles after charity and duty to one's neighbour, as though beating a drum in search of a fugitive. Alas! Sir, you have brought much confusion into the mind of man."[2]

Figure 1.2. Confucius and Lao-tzu in dialogue
By Jiwon Kim

In this imaginary dialogue, Lao-tzu reiterates that if we interfere in the natural process of any living organism, it will begin to isolate itself from the complementary parts of the whole. This isolation brings about a disassociation from the whole, so that a lack of trust plagues the mind.

Confucius's ideas of charity and duty to one's neighbor are age-old teachings, which artists, philosophers, and spiritual teachers have contemplated from the dawn of civilization to the present day. On the surface, we may all feel convinced that he is correct in postulating that we have a duty to others. But the Taoist Way of Lao-tzu suggests that in attempting to interfere with others' affairs, no matter how large or small, we are assuming that the natural experience of life is not happening spontaneously; instead we think that life is a series of controlled steps following a predictable and mechanical process. Lao-tzu is not saying that we should abolish duty or charity. He is saying that everything in the universe is integral and symbiotic in nature, and that everything functions harmoniously according to the rhythm of the universe. So, he asks, why would humanity be the exception? The Way of the Tao and our experience of it comes from allowing all aspects of the universe to happen as they will without conscious interference.

This understanding of Tao is a trust in and affirmation of life that cannot be broken. Humanity's superficial differences could be dissolved if each individual could live by this trust. Yet society and culture have been built on ideologies such as Confucianism, communism, and democracy, which all teach us in some way to impose our will over one another, a goal based on the erroneous idea that we are achieving freedom in this process. To trust the Way of the Tao is the complete backflip to Confucianism or any present-day ideology or theology. Lao-tzu's wisdom exposes humanity's selfish tendency to impose the will of one individual, nation, religion, race, or gender over another. We are always interfering with each other's natural sovereignty. Many people arrogantly and ignorantly do this daily and then proclaim that they know what freedom and love are. How can we listen and help each other if it is merely from our own cultural, social, or religious perspective? If we have a set of beliefs to sell another, then we are surely imposing our idea of life upon her without letting her grow as nature intended.

It is this personal agenda that Lao-tzu reveals. If we interfere unnecessarily with any organism on this planet, we hinder its growth through our attempt to control it. When it is interfered with, an organism finds itself in a struggle to grow into everything it should be. As a result, the organism's natural impulse to grow is met with resistance by another organism, which assumes that it is superior to all life and needs no other organisms to survive. We could say human beings fit perfectly into this category because of the personal agendas we wish to cast upon the world. These agendas could only have developed in a world devoid of trust. Because we live in fear instead of trust, our world is designed so clinically that it resembles not a beautiful garden but a morgue.

The Confucian imperative to dictate a social way of life to the individual builds an identity conditioned by the world of concepts and objects rather than the inner world of emotions, feelings, and thoughts. Yet we should not be critical of the Confucian perspective only, because any ideology or theology, no matter how well intended, is at its foundation strictly a methodology for shaping the individual according to its beliefs. Lao-tzu points to this in the *Tao Te Ching*. He says that humanity is in a perpetual trap in which we seek to change one another or society based on our own belief systems. Because we have not made our inner world conscious, we continue to seek change in the external world of forms, as if the inner world were a construct of the outer. Many theologies and ideologies operate from this perspective. But this is an absurd view for the simple reason that the world is devoid of meaning until the observer gives it meaning according to her beliefs. This should be fundamental to the way we think and perceive the world. But instead we are told that the world is purely material by the teachers of our cultural, social, religious, and educational machine, who themselves have been indoctrinated.

To cultivate a sane society, we first need to understand that our perception was pure before it was colored by external influences. And all of these external influences are interpreted differently by each individual, which adds to the confusion. Patanjali, the great sage of India and father of yoga, expresses this sentiment in the wisdom of three of his sutras regarding freedom:

> *People perceive the same object differently, as each person's perception follows a separate path from another's.*

> *But the object is not dependent on either of those perceptions; if it were, what would happen to it when nobody was looking?*

An object is known only by a consciousness it has colored;
otherwise it is not known.[3]

We have built a world that operates in reverse to the natural order of growth and harmonious living. The world's general view identifies with what colors consciousness rather than with the unbound and limitless pure awareness at the core of our being. Lao-tzu's essential teaching of wu-wei is a medicine for this illness.

But you must understand that wu-wei is not an ideology, theology, or something you need to believe in. On the contrary, wu-wei can only be known through your own experience. Then it simply strengthens your trust in wu-wei. The natural order of growth and harmony depends upon allowing life to take its course without conscious interference. This is how the Tao flows when wu-wei is experienced. Many people resist the very thought of allowing things to take place in life, because from our perspective we can't see how anything could be achieved in that way. But if we are more observant, we discover that each and every attempt to categorically control our life is invariably upended by the spontaneity of natural experience. No human being is above this universal spontaneity. And yet many people seek to control life down to the finest detail, failing to realize that the very things that shaped their identity were beyond their control.

THE PHANTOMS OF CONTROL
AND SECURITY

Pain comes when the control we think we have comes crashing down in the light of reality. We fail to realize that the ability to imagine is a vehicle we use to try and control our future. These future projections may be pleasurable, but usually these pleasurable experiences do not come to fruition. Yet we cringe at the reality of living completely in the here and now.

Control is nothing more than an attempt to bring the past and future under our command. Our personal agendas are secret ways of trying to control the destiny of others based on the memories of our past. The pure, natural awareness of our consciousness is polluted by the illusion that we can control each and every situation in life. Spontaneity is loathed by many people; it conflicts with their incessant control. The transformation of Lao-tzu's Taoism into Confucianism is no different.

Lao-tzu exemplifies the rebel in the truest sense of the word, because, following the effortless grace of wu-wei, he is uninterested in worldly affairs. The Taoist Way is not to lord it over anything or anyone. All aspects of nature are allowed to run their course without interference. Sometimes, however, skillful guidance can be given by those who have realized the Tao and function according to wu-wei. But when we unskillfully attempt to tell another individual what to do, how to think, or how to be, we are in fact destroying that individual. Parents are the best example. They project their own idea of the world onto their children without letting them follow their own interests. Parents in such a state of control do not love their children unconditionally. On the contrary, they want for their children what is acceptable in the eyes of the society and world. In this way, we treat children as meaningless material objects. And yet this model is accepted as parenting par excellence.

This vicious cycle of hypnotic parenting can only manifest in a society and culture that have stripped the trust in life out of people. In one sense, our parents are not to blame. But on the other hand, they *are* to blame, because like everyone else in this world, they are naturally sovereign and have a responsibility to avoid imposing their agendas onto others. In this case a family becomes the microcosm of the society in which it dwells. Parents become hierarchical tyrants who terrorize their children with indoctrination. When an ideology, such as democracy or Confucianism, imposes its idea of life upon our minds, we begin a lifelong journey of suppressing our natural inclinations and the creative expression for freedom. This suppression strangles the innate power that we all possess. And when we lose our innate power, we seek to project it into avenues that we feel comfortable in controlling.

All types of personal relationships exhibit this constant game of one-upmanship. It's not only evident in parents and children but can be found in intimate relationships, such as those between husband and wife. There is always a constant battle for power; each party is trying to make the other yield to his own idea of how life should be. They are attracted to power because society is based on an artificial system that teaches the individual to chase material comforts and convenience in the belief that this will bring security. Our indoctrination teaches us that the more possessions we have, the more powerful and successful we are, and power lies in what is used to acquire these possessions. The symbol of power in our world is money. Yet money itself is empty and valueless until we give it value. We discover that this is true when we realize that the wealthiest people on this planet are usually the unhappiest.

The impulse to control life is a symptom of the power that we believe we have lost. But true power resides in the mind of one who is liberated from the acquisition of wealth and the control of others. When we give up attempting to control life, we find that we are no longer clinging to or conditioned by any aspect of life. Thus we are freed from its attachments. The most liberated people on this planet have been those who were free in this way, such as the twentieth-century Indian sage Sri Ramana Maharshi.

THE SUPERIOR MAN

Confucius audaciously tried to bring morality and ethics into the consciousness of humanity with his concept of the superior man, known as *junzi* (君子: Wade-Giles *chün-tzu,* Pinyin *junzi*) in Chinese. Keep in mind that although the Taoist perspective uses the term *superior man* to refer to both men and women, this is not the case in Confucianism, because Confucius was not overly confident in women's ability to attain wisdom. *Superior man,* according to Confucius, literally meant *man.* Indeed his view of the superior man is that of a man who acts outwardly in a cultured and learned manner, very much like the English concept of the gentleman. Nevertheless, Confucius did point out that a man of any social class could be a superior man if he cultivates the virtues of ju in his character.

Here is where Confucius and Lao-tzu's views of the superior man differ: Confucius believes that we are naturally born with rough edges; we are almost beastlike. As a result, we need to chisel away at our being to mold it into a human shape. This is his philosophy of "carving and polishing." Lao-tzu, on the other hand, believed that we are naturally pure; it is the belief systems and social indoctrination of the world that give us a gross character and warp our pure nature. As a result, we need to get back to the raw, intrinsically human, elements of our being. This is known as returning to the "uncarved block" or "unhewn wood." Lao-tzu's teaching of wu-wei is not a method of telling the individual how to be *like* the superior man, but instead it gives the individual the knowledge of how to *become* the superior man.

An individual with an effortless mind resulting from the practice of wu-wei travels with the stream to its source, which is the ocean of Tao. When we attempt to control life, we are assuming that we do not belong to the universe, so we begin to drown in the current of change. This lack of trust in the universe comes from the way we orient our perception toward the world. In believing that external influences control life, we have a psychological tendency to worship those influences. We become bound by what comes through our senses. This breeds artificiality, because the individual worships what is conceptual.

2

The Way of Nature Is No Religion or Dogma

The goal of all spiritual paths is to liberate us from our conditioned perception of things as separate. When we are liberated from this perception of life, we will merge with the one God/Godhead/Tao/Brahman that is found within all of us when we go beyond our conditioned thoughts, feelings, and emotions. The very word *religion* comes from the Latin *religare,* "to bind," and means union with the ultimate source of consciousness that we have conceptualized as God. Comparable to the word *religion* is *yoga,* which comes from the Sanskrit root word *yuj.* This again means "union" with the ultimate mystery we call God. This union is the metaphysical truth spoken of in all religious doctrine.

SAVE THE WORLD FROM WHOM?

The concept of collective awakening is a New Age phantom created from the illusion that our world somehow needs to be saved. This is exactly the same premise by which dogmatic organized religions were established. The idea that the world needs to be saved is contradicted by the fact that no one can ever explain from whom or what we are saving the world, largely because we are attempting to save the world from ourselves. I am not speaking about the real *you* in this context, as the real *you* is beyond name and form. Rather we are attempting to save the world from our own personality or ego. This ego aspect of oneself is only acquired through the conditioning of life, which binds us to endless desires and suffering that push our civilization, and our planet, piece by piece into devolution.

The idea of saving the world is merely intellectual speculation based on our own personal agendas. This does not mean that poverty and ecological crisis don't exist. But it does mean that the world begins to suffer, internally and externally, when we identify solely with the ego, which is attracted to constant moving and doing at the expense of stillness and nondoing (yang over yin). The ground of our being at the heart of stillness is untouched by the fluctuations of matter and energy within the physical and mental planes of consciousness. Who we truly are deep down is beyond the constraints of change. Who we truly are at the ground of our being is a resonance with the metaphysical truth that underlies the phenomenal universe. Even though many people yearn to experience union in this life, it is absurd to believe that we will one day undergo some sort of collective awakening. The phenomenal world of change functions in accordance with the rhythm and vibration of consciousness, which differs according to the attunement of the individual components. We are these individual components.

The collective evolution of consciousness into a higher metaphysical state would oppose the constant unfolding of organic life on Earth. For organic life on Earth, it is necessary that all of its components be harmonious with the planetary forces that support nature's growth.

Humanity makes up a part of those harmonious components. If the entire human population were to awaken collectively to the formless truth beyond forms, would this benefit organic life or be catastrophic for it? Is it really possible? The Greco-Armenian mystic George Ivanovich Gurdjieff discusses individual and collective evolution in the book *In Search of the Miraculous,* by the Russian mathematician and esotericist P. D. Ouspensky:

> The evolution of large masses of humanity is opposed to nature's purposes. The evolution of a certain small percentage may be in accord with nature's purposes. Man contains within him the possibility of evolution. But the evolution of humanity as a whole, that is, the development of these possibilities in all men, or in most of them, or even in a large number of them, is not necessary for the purposes of the earth or of the planetary world in general, and it might, in fact, be injurious or fatal.
>
> But, at the same time, possibilities of evolution exist, and they may be developed in *separate* individuals with the help of appropriate knowledge and methods. Such development can take place only in the interests of the man himself against, so to speak, the interests and forces of the planetary world. The man must understand this: his evolution is necessary only to himself. No one else is interested in it. And no one is obliged or intends to help him. On the contrary, the forces which oppose the evolution of large masses of humanity also oppose the evolution of individual men. A man must outwit them. And *one* man can outwit them, humanity *cannot.* You will understand later on that all these obstacles are very useful to a man; if they did not exist they would have to be created intentionally, because it is by overcoming obstacles that man develops those qualities he needs.
>
> This is the basis of the correct view of human evolution. There is no compulsory, mechanical evolution. Evolution is the result of

conscious struggle. Nature does not need this evolution; it does not want it and struggles against it. Evolution can be necessary only to man himself when he realizes his position, realizes the possibility of changing this position, realizes that he has powers that he does not use, riches that he does not see. And, in the sense of gaining possession of these powers and riches, evolution is possible. But if *all men,* or most of them, realized this and desired to obtain what belongs to them by right of birth, evolution would again become impossible. What is possible for individual man is impossible for the masses.[1]

Lao-tzu's Taoist philosophy was not promoting a sort of medicine for the world's ills. He understood that the world's ills are cured only by the liberation, or in other words evolution, of the individual. Lao-tzu was not concerned with a collective awakening but with living in harmony with the universe. In his eyes, awakening does not depend on anything other than your own realization of the metaphysical truth, the irreducible essence, that he called *Tao.*

Because Tao is something we become conscious of from our experience, it is insufficient to try to verbalize or point to Tao categorically, especially for those who have not deepened their awareness within themselves. Because Tao is not bound to a moment of experience, it continues to unfold in those who are centered within their own inner world. This is why ancient Eastern masters regard Tao, or God, as a verb rather than as a noun. From this point of view, Tao gets deeper as one marinates one's being more and more in the union with that eternal truth.

The experience of Tao in life is never the same for each individual. The depth of understanding is always expanding. *That* which is the source of Tao is the same within all human beings. Our personality becomes more refined as we explore its depths more and more until the Tao is our complete center of gravity. The spiritual profundity of Tao is focused on the irreducible essence of the universe within each and every one of us. This irreducible essence is and can only be known by the individual, not the collective. But our world is oriented around the false assumption that the Tao is harnessed, and it is shaped by the belief that the external world influences the internal world of the individual. With such a view, the Taoist Way of Lao-tzu becomes an organized system that one should follow in the hope of becoming enlightened in relation to a social structure. This view of Lao-tzu's Tao was eventually given systemic form by Confucius. In attempting to embed Taoism within society, Confucius largely contributed to Taoism becoming what it is not: a religion.

CONFUCIAN ROOTS
OF RELIGIOUS TAOISM

Lao-tzu was not setting out a religion to follow, or an ideology or theology to live by. He understood that the Tao can only be known through experience; it cannot be explained through doctrine, nor can it be invented or induced through a practice. Yet the Taoism that was established after Lao-tzu is commonly known as a religion. If his Way eventually became one of these systems of belief, it must have come down through others who tampered with it or completely misinterpreted it.

This Taoist religion is more Confucian than Taoist. Confucius sought to give form to the formless Tao. This may have been the right thing to do for the society of his time. But even Confucius could not have predicted that the mystery within his ideology could become a form of religion.

Mistaking Taoism for a religion has kept many sincere spiritual seekers away from the depth and freedom of the Way because of its association with religious dogma. Many people who are sincerely exploring their own inner world tend to shy away from organized religion, because many religions lay out a dogmatic path rather than providing the tools for liberation.

Lao-tzu's *Tao Te Ching* is obviously not a statement of religious doctrine or dogma; rather it is a universal song about the Way/Tao that brings space into the inner world of an individual, aligning her with the universe's nature and evolutionary process. But astonishingly, the *religion* of Taoism elaborated upon Lao-tzu's spiritual text and constructed a whole set of beliefs and dogmas around it. Again, these beliefs and dogmas are more in alignment with Confucianism than with Lao-tzu's original Taoist path. This Taoism is focused on reverencing ancestors and spirits through rites and rituals. But centering wholeheartedly on the phenomenal world orients an individual toward seeking good fortune in this life instead of following and knowing Tao.

Taoism in this sense is often confused with Chinese folk religion because of their outward similarities, including the veneration of and sometimes communication with ancestors; teachings about energetic streams such as *qi* (Wade-Giles *ch'i*, Pinyin *qi*) or "life energy"; and emphasis on the physical phenomena of the sun, moon, Earth, heaven, stars, and galaxies. Observing both the religion of Taoism and Chinese folk religion, we are dazzled by their colors and their parade of rituals and ceremonies. Indeed the Taoist religion is built around ancestral worship, ritual, and sacrifice.

Yet according to Lao-tzu, these are nothing but mere distractions from the Absolute Tao, which is eternally *now* and is discovered in living a simple life. Even though ancestral spirits and nature spirits may exist, Lao-tzu perceived them as part of the Tao of things, distracting our attention away from establishing harmony with the Absolute Tao. When we focus our attention on ancestors who have long since passed from the body, we are conjuring up emotions of the past and memories that in the end only distract us from the Tao. We can never fully embrace the Tao and be in its flow *now* unless we let the dead rest in peace.

THE LOST MEANING OF RITUAL

In Asia there is an overemphasis on ancestral worship. Once upon a time it may have been a genuine sacred practice, but in the modern day it has turned into dogma. To be constantly looking into the past to worship our ancestors is to cling to the past and, in doing so, to swim against the stream of Tao. To know the Tao means understanding that all life returns to the one source, and so all manifest things, which are from that source, are one. How could we worship ancestors as if they were separate from that source? The argument from traditional Eastern philosophy is that the ancestor we are worshipping is only the ephemeral personality, for which we have affection, rather than the actual Eternal Self that resides in that individual. Our worship, then, is attuned to our personal perception of the ancestors, which is only the idea we have of them, and so it is unfortunately an empty exercise.

The natural Eternal Self is one with the Tao as the Tao. In the Hindu philosophy of Vedanta (*Vedanta* literally means *end of the Vedas* and refers to teachings based on the three source texts, the *Upanishads,* the *Bhagavad Gita,* and the *Brahma Sutras,* with all three collectively known as *Prasthanatrayi*), the deep down *real you* is the entire universe. The *Atman* (Eternal Self/undifferentiated consciousness) is the *Brahman* (ultimate reality beyond knowing), but we have forgotten that we are Brahman in the same way that we forget where we put our keys. If this is our reality, then our worship could not be divided up according to separate individuals who have died. Lao-tzu's feelings on clinging to the worship of ancestors is best summed up by a conversation between Micayon and Mirdad in *The Book of Mirdad,* the masterpiece by the Lebanese author and poet Mikhail Naimy:

Micayon: Would you not tell us who you are? Perhaps, if we knew your name—your real name—your country and your ancestry we would the better understand you.

Mirdad: Ah, Micayon! As well force an eagle back into the shell out of which he hatched as try to chain Mirdad with your chains and veil him in your veils. What name can ever designate a Man who is no longer "in the shell"? What country can contain a Man in whom an universe is contained? What ancestry can claim a Man whose only ancestor is God?[2]

Contrary to Lao-tzu, Confucius said that ancestral worship, ritual, and sacrifice are necessary for social harmony. This again takes the focus away from the individual, as the society takes pride of place. But this should be no surprise, as we could describe Confucianism as a sociopolitical doctrine having religious qualities. Even though Lao-tzu's philosophy had a great bearing upon Confucius, Confucius could not embrace it totally, because Confucianism is primarily built on more ancient animistic and shamanic traditions in Chinese culture. Yet the rituals and ceremonies that we still have today from those ancient times have lost their meaning and significance. Both Lao-tzu and Confucius lived during the Zhou dynasty (1046–256 BCE), when the rites and rituals, though still the primary focus of worship, lost all meaning. (In the earlier Shang dynasty [1600–1046 BCE], rites and rituals were aimed at the unseen spirit world and toward their own sense of Tao.)

Amazingly, the religion of Taoism continues to practice the ancestral worship, ritual, and sacrifice of Confucianism even though few individuals have a deep understanding of why these rites are practiced in the first place. The Taoist religion and Confucianism are built tightly around a rigid tradition that has not fundamentally changed its shape since the time of Confucius. As the individual and the world continue to evolve, these traditions lose their significance, as the collective consciousness has evolved far past the epoch of time to which they belonged. (This is not to say that Confucianism has lost its moral and ethical significance in the modern world.)

Lao-tzu's Tao, on the other hand, is a mystery that belongs to no tradition or religion. It is discovered in the depth of our being in the same way that Atman is Brahman in Vedanta. The Tao of Lao-tzu is that eternal principle which we cannot fathom intellectually because it is beyond the mental framework of time and space. Beyond the world of form is the source of Tao, and those who choose to know it by following its synchronistic pull will grow out of the mud into beautiful lotus flowers. These individuals have a relationship with the Tao, and they shine brightly through their creativity and humility, as both virtues have merged in kinship under the universal guidance of Tao.

NATURE'S REBEL IS SOCIETY'S THREAT

The virtuous individual always presents danger to social, religious, and cultural systems that seek to bind humanity with superficial constraints. The individual who knows and follows the Tao is a threat because his way of being is liberated from the shackles of external influence. From the cultural, religious, and social perspective, these individuals are rebels who threaten to disrupt the hypnosis of the status quo. This is why we see the unceremonious killing of such figures who know and follow Tao, such as Jesus of Nazareth (no matter whether you take the story of Jesus to be real or metaphor).

True and eternal freedom is loathed by the tyrants of cultural, ideological, theological, social, and religious dogmas, because when we are liberated by the true freedom that we can only find within us, we cease to conform to the machinations of tyranny. Artists, mystics, philosophers, scientists, and the spiritually inclined all exhibit this exalted state through their own creativity and humility, which often exposes the flaws of a system that seeks to dictate to the masses. The rebellion of Lao-tzu's Taoist Way has always posed a threat to the established order, especially in China. True Taoism was suppressed in the first decades of the People's Republic of China (with people even persecuted during the Cultural Revolution), though it continued to be practiced in Taiwan. Taoism has often been scorned because the essential Taoist teaching of wu-wei is about surrendering your life into the comforting arms and the Way of the universe rather than conforming to social ethics. The Absolute Tao is the prerogative of the original Taoist. But this sincerity is confusing to any established order, because the Tao of Lao-tzu is as vast as it is vague, and so it escapes conventional thought and behavior.

An authentic Taoist is often thought of as a soothsayer or witch, because our world seeks to find definitions for everything. This absurd definition gives the masses some sort of psychological closure, as if they now somehow understood Tao. But what Lao-tzu and other Taoists knew within themselves is beyond intellectual debate or conjecture. This eternal *truth,* known only by some people, frustrates those who know it not. In the eyes of an established ideology, theology, or organized religion, this experiential truth disrupts the social indoctrination that keeps the masses moving to the beat of someone else's drum. This is one of the main reasons why Lao-tzu's Tao conflicts with Confucius's ideology. Lao-tzu understood that any form of social or cultural hierarchy destroys the awareness of trust in the universe. Confucius could not accept this, because his approach was only for those who governed. He thought if those who governed were liberated and morally noble, society would benefit.

In truth, this view is not oriented toward the freedom of the individual; rather it is a clever system devised to manage society without the people of that society questioning their position. Democracy is similar. The ideology of democracy tries to maintain a society's comfort and convenience based on liberal views, so that the bigger questions of life are never asked of those imposing democracy upon the people. The hierarchical systems of governments, banking, corporations, and royalty end up becoming tyrants rather than servants. Yet according to Lao-tzu, if any system is devised to control anything, then we have ceased to follow the Way of nature. Then control invariably turns into a selfish and corrupting urge to lord it over others. As John Dalberg-Acton, the English Catholic historian, politician, and writer, wrote in 1887, "Power tends to corrupt, and absolute power corrupts absolutely. Great men are almost always bad men."[3]

Selfish power has corrupted the world with the belief that we can control life within a fixed reality that is devoid of spontaneity. Evolution, on the other hand, means pushing the limitations of our minds and the traditional boundaries we have constructed. Confucianism, the religion of Taoism, and other religious traditions are being tested in the modern era. Their dogmas have become exhausted, and the world is becoming attuned to an authentic spirituality, as a new awareness of ourselves in relation to each other, the world, and the universe is developing.

Tradition is not intrinsically bad, and many traditions can be beautiful. But they lose this beauty, and they become psychologically damaging, when they set up dogmas to imprison the mind. We only have to look at modern-day Christianity for an example. The Way of Lao-tzu was to never be attached to any tradition that imprisoned our mind because if we hold our center within, we will move with the evolutionary energies of the universe without resistance. These evolutionary energies materialize as synchronicity on the level of the conscious mind.

Though traditions may come and go, their remnants sometimes linger within the collective consciousness for some time. The continent of Asia is a good example, because even though the ideology of Confucianism is often unacknowledged as a prevailing system of thought, the dogmatic beliefs of that socioeconomic religious ideology still keep people from embracing change. These dogmas are bringing tenseness and frustration into the lives of the common people, because the collective consciousness has evolved past such rigid traditions, much as we are evolving past the vain materialism of the West and its attempts to shove liberalism down everybody's throat. Consciousness is dancing to a new rhythm and vibration, both collectively and individually.

FILIAL PIETY AND THE OPPRESSED INDIVIDUAL

Confucian dogmas promote inequality not only within the society but also within families. Parents following Confucian dogma often become tyrants over their children, as if there should be an unquestionable respect and obedience by children for parents. But is this mode of authority love for one's children? Are we not still lording it over the naturalness of our children? Of course the answer is yes, but Confucian indoctrination blinds one to that fact. This code of conduct is known as "filial piety," *xiao* (孝: Wade-Giles *hsiao,* Pinyin *xiao*) in Chinese.

The Chinese tradition of filial piety existed before both Confucius and Lao-tzu, and it has always been considered a high virtue in Chinese culture. It makes up a large part of Confucius's general teaching of obedience to those who are perceived as superior. The *Classic of Filial Piety,* or *Xiao Jing* in Chinese, attributed to Confucius, has a conversation between him and his student Zeng Zi about the way to set up a moral and ethical society based on the principle of filial piety. Confucius says, "In serving his parents, a filial son reveres them in daily life; he makes them happy while he nourishes them; he takes anxious care of them in sickness; he shows great sorrow over their death; and he sacrifices to them with solemnity."[4]

Though this may make it appear that the son has an underlying love for his parents, it is in truth quite the opposite. From the day we are born up until the age of twelve or thirteen, we develop a psychological dependency on our parents and society. Some tribal cultures acknowledge and try to overcome this dependency. In some New Guinea tribes, a child at the age of twelve or thirteen is put into battle against an elder, who is masked as a god. This whole battle symbolizes the child's breaking free from his chains of dependency with parents and tribe. The child wins the battle, which reveals to him that he has become a complete individual, free from dependency on the past.

Confucius was wrong to assume that subservient children would produce superior people, because their disposition is always taken from the inferior psychological state of dependency. This subservient dependency is especially rife in countries such as China, Japan, Cambodia, North Korea, South Korea, Thailand, and Vietnam, where Confucian dogmas are still held in high regard. When one is in these nations, one senses an underlying feeling of oppression as a result of Confucian tradition.

By contrast, Lao-tzu believed that our individual and collective oppression was fueled by our sense of inferiority through assumed dependency. This dependency, according to the old master, only benefits the systemic beliefs of any social and cultural ideology because it strengthens their illusory boundaries. Lao-tzu alludes to this paradox in chapter 18 of the *Tao Te Ching*:

> *When the great Tao is forgotten,*
> *goodness and piety appear.*
> *When the body's intelligence declines,*
> *cleverness and knowledge step forth.*
> *When there is no peace in the family,*
> *filial piety begins.*
> *When the country falls into chaos,*
> *patriotism is born.*[5]

Confucianism thus builds an overly conservative society, always in fear of change and outside influence. The youth of such societies often question the dogmas they are supposed to uphold, but usually over time the culture wears them down to lifeless entities. Yet some do slip through the cracks and become independent, such as South Korean writer Kim Kyong-il, who wrote the controversial book *Confucius Must Die for the Nation to Live*. He discusses how Confucianism's outdated traditions are causing a bipolar effect within the individual, which leads to a flavorless and suppressed society. He says that government keeps forcing Confucian filial obligations upon families, and as a result no individual ever questions the government's authority, because their sense of filial piety makes them feel inferior.

Filial piety is one-sided and blind. It is a way of maintaining inequality among humanity, as the senior is wrongly assumed to be the superior. But, from an evolutionary perspective, those who are still bound by such traditions are resisting the flow of Tao. Thus they are truly inferior. In this context, the superior individuals must be the youth, because they are challenging tradition in order to change and evolve. Their beliefs have not sunk their roots deep within their mind, and so they are less heavily conditioned.

This type of inequality is not limited to Asia. To different degrees, it is still prevalent all around the world. For example, many cultures imply or state that young people should always respect their elders. Yet doesn't this mentality indoctrinate inferiority? Why shouldn't elders show respect toward the youth? Instead of respecting the young, elders often show an arrogant contempt toward them, as if they do not know what life is about. But what life is about according to the majority of elders is turning the mind into a rigid stone by means of tradition. How could we trust an elder who functions from such a premise?

Contrary to this attitude, in many indigenous tribes we find a reverence expressed by elders for the young. They know that tribal life can only flourish when all people of the tribe are held as equal. Human equality cannot be achieved by any system or individual imposing their will over the natural sovereignty of other individuals.

Inequality of the sexes has been noticeable within many societies, religions, and cultures. Yet over the last hundred years we have seen women prove that this notion of female inferiority is false. Women continue to break free of the traditional prison of filial piety and lead the way out of these dogmas. If we can accept that women are not inferior (as our civilization appears to be doing), why is it so hard to assume that our children should not also have equal status?

The Confucian control of the future and its traditions of the past will always drown in the spontaneous flow of the Tao. Wu-wei is not a way of controlling the future by projecting the past onto it. On the contrary, it is to live spontaneously *now* so that we know how to live in the future.

3

The Way of the Tao
Is Harmony

The great sage Chuang-tzu, who was absorbed in the wisdom of Lao-tzu, found it quite perplexing to see how the civilization of his time gave name and form to the philosophy of that which is beyond name and form. Chuang-tzu lived in the classical period of Chinese philosophy known as the "Hundred Schools of Thought" (諸子百家), which flourished from the sixth century BCE to 221 BCE, during the Spring and Autumn period (771–476 BCE) and the Warring States period (475–221 BCE) of ancient China. Unlike Lao-tzu, Chuang-tzu's existence can be verified. In that classical period, he was at the heart of an epoch of change that was sweeping across humanity.

This epoch is almost identical to our present day, where unbelievable changes are taking place whether we like it or not. Something is compelling humanity to grow out of a dysfunctional state into a harmonious one. Everything in our current epoch is either decaying or transforming in much the same way as in Chuang-tzu's time. Ideologies, theologies, religions, and culture all underwent a radical change. The beliefs that were not open to change evaporated like snow on a summer's day. Chuang-tzu knew that it was the Tao that changes something spontaneously out of its extreme rigidity. The Tao through Chuang-tzu's eyes is within everything, not just the movements of the bodies or seasons, but also within the transformation of human civilizations and the new patterns of thought that give birth to them. Out of spontaneity an evolutionary burst of energy takes place, because spontaneity is the Way of nature. So evolution in relation to humanity is the spontaneous growth of consciousness.

These bursts of expansive growth within the collective consciousness are scattered all throughout history. If Chuang-tzu could speak to us, he would add that these epochs can be dangerous because of incorrect guidance through misinterpretation. This danger is evident in our present day, as we see how the Tao of Lao-tzu has been deformed by rigid traditions that have lost sight of its inner meaning, not to mention the misinterpretation of Eastern philosophy as New Age nonsense.

This classical period of Chinese philosophy saw the universal text of the *Tao Te Ching* come into existence to explain the Way, which is discovered by few. But by the time Chuang-tzu was touched by its depth, the *Tao Te Ching* had been molded and shaped into a medicine for the society rather than the individual. Confucian ideals and older animistic and shamanic traditions nurtured and then cloaked the Tao. Chuang-tzu could perceive this, but he met such peculiarities with humor and sarcasm. Being absorbed in the Way of the Tao, he was naturally disinterested in anything culture, religion, or society could offer, and as a result he found great joy in poking fun at its temporality. Similarly, today we discover a multitude of individuals who are waking up to the frivolousness of the society, culture, and religions we have built.

When our consciousness evolves, what we once couldn't perceive or imagine soon becomes perceivable and then becomes direct knowledge.

How could this be if we are to accept the conventional model of linear evolution? The mechanical linear model of the universe is the common, indoctrinated perspective on life. But there is no categorical evidence to support this view. The laws of nature do not follow a linear model. All forms of life in nature grow spontaneously into a design of differing distinguished patterns that all fit together. Spontaneity is the essence of patterned structures within nature, which work harmoniously together in a common union. This perspective encompasses Lao-tzu's wisdom that the Tao is the Way of nature.

Nature's constituents are inseparable and arise out of the Tao, which gives the differing aspects of nature their energetic signatures in the form of complex patterns. The Tao dwells deep within the pattern of the form that has spontaneously arisen. Perceiving the Tao in nature is an accomplishment of the enlightened sages. Chuang-tzu once stated, "When there is no more separation between 'this' and 'that,' it is called the still-point of the Tao. At the still-point in the center of the circle one can see the infinite in all things."[1]

Chuang-tzu could have only attained this enlightened perception from following the Way of nature. His life was in accord with the Tao. In this alignment the Tao nourishes one who is of its original essence. Chuang-tzu's humor is a testament to his own natural spontaneity. Those who have revealed Lao-tzu's Way of nature in their own lives stand back in awe at the complexity of the linear system we have built in opposition to nature's rhythm. The nonlinear world of natural organisms are harmonious within their own patterned design, even though these patterns conflict with our linear worldview.

THE ORGANIC PATTERN OF LI

There is an organic pattern, or we could say order of the universe, that is a blueprint for nature to express its beauty. In Chinese this is called *li* (理; see figure 3.1), which I briefly mentioned in the introduction.

Li is usually translated as the markings in jade, grain in wood, and fiber in muscle. It is supposed to signify a definite pattern that originates within an organism as its nature and comes into existence when an organism harmonizes with the Tao. This li principle is usually thought of as Neo-Confucian rather than Taoist, because it differs from the Confucian virtue of *li* (禮), which is based on correct understanding and practice of rites and ceremonies. The Confucian concept of li has no relevance to the Way of Lao-tzu or to the harmony of nature. Nor is it relevant to wu-wei. Nature exhibits the Taoist li (理) always, as the mineral, plant, and animal kingdoms are not intelligences that could try to disrupt its harmony. The human kingdom, on the other hand, being the highest form of intelligence on this planet, constantly seeks to challenge nature's laws and rhythms.

Humanity has a schizoid sense that we are somehow alien to this planet. Yet we depend on nature for everything that gives us life. Without the food that we eat or the air that we breathe, we would not have evolved out of the lower kingdoms. We feel alienated from all other life because we perceive only a linear world. From this convoluted view, we build our communities on linear systems. The society is a construct of designed systems, such as organized culture, government, politics, and religion, which all oppose natural laws and swim against the current of Tao.

We erroneously uphold these systems because we feel that life

Figure 3.1. Li—universal organic pattern
By Dao Stew

would be nothing without them. Yet they are built on the notion that we can control nature's pattern, li. The destruction of nature for material gain is a result of these systems' effect on the human mind. We pay more attention to our own indoctrination than to the actual world that gives us life. Nature, being nonlinear, cannot be understood by a humanity shaped by a linear perspective. From this standpoint, we seek to lord it over nature because we do not understand it. Yet according to Lao-tzu and Chuang-tzu, this is the very problem that will lead us into complete and utter annihilation, because in not understanding nature, we do not understand ourselves.

The Tao that Chuang-tzu could perceive in everything does not exclude human life. Human life is an intrinsic part of nature because a human being *is* nature. The fight for control of nature stems from humanity ignoring its own nature, which we do when we adopt external influences that transform us into machines. Our psychology in turn resembles the repetition of a machine rather than the spontaneity of nature.

The mind of the average individual is solely focused on the maintenance and upkeep of a linear system. Such a person is unlikely to allocate any energy toward her own inner world, because that would conflict with her linear habits. But this orientation toward the outer world is going to lead us into the arms of annihilation if we do not realize that all natural growth comes from within the organism. And all of nature's constituents, including human beings, function according to this universal pattern. Nature's harmony can be disturbed but never eradicated, because the Tao courses through the patterns of li. Organisms that challenge this order do not fare well.

We generally ignore the fact that the organic pattern and principle of li are within the human organism too. The organic pattern of li within the ecosystem is the same intelligence that is found in our nerves, senses, and ultimately our cognitive functions and psychology. This is why those who practice spiritual cultivation usually have a harmonious biological and psychological disposition: they show respect to their bodies and minds by refusing to overstimulate them with excessive consumption. The Taoist philosophy of li affirms that anyone can attain a liberated state of harmony with the world, but only if we act in the same way as nature. The ecosystem of nature is nothing like the average modern life of a human being. What, then, would it take for a human to act as nature intended?

Nature's Way is harmonious because each of its components follows its own li, its way of harmonizing with other manifestations of Tao. This mutual resonance and interdependence is known as *ying* (應: Wade-Giles *ying,* Pinyin *ying,* see figure 3.2) in Chinese, and is another key aspect of Taoist philosophy. It is an essential principle for understanding the effortless mind. The mutual resonance and harmony of nature are only possible in the way they are as the Tao is.

When we look into nature, we do not see the busyness and complexity of, say, a city. On the contrary, we perceive a simple world in harmony through the stillness of Tao. Chuang-tzu said that from the still point of the Tao in the center of the circle, one can see the infinite in the world of forms. This means that the mind that is completely empty and still can perceive reality as it truly *is.* The Tao liberates the mind from its linear constraints by enabling it to follow the Way of nature.

Figure 3.2. Ying—mutual resonance and interdependence
By Dao Stew

To act according to nature requires becoming receptive to the forces of the cosmos, which can only be received in the complete stilling of the mind. The process of settling the ripples of the mind is known as *nirodha* in Sanskrit, which in Patanjali's classical yoga means "restriction," the process of stopping the "whirls" (*vritti* in Sanskrit) of the mind. This stilling of the mind is the key objective of many forms of meditative practices and Eastern wisdom. Yet, paradoxically, the objective can never be attained if it is thought of as a goal to achieve. This is because the stillness of mind that many people hope to attain is actually our natural state right *here and now* and not at some future destination. But this realization is veiled by the hypnosis that we have acquired from the external world.

Enlightenment right *here and now* is the sage's axiom. A sage would ask us, how could we ever attain or achieve something that is already our true nature? This may look simple for sages to realize, but keep in mind that they were also once on a journey of self-discovery. They too had to undergo the process of thinning out their conditioned personality so that they could ultimately recognize that consciousness is naturally transparent and reflective like water.

Water acts in the same way as mind. When water is disturbed, it is not transparent or reflective, as the waves and ripples obscure its essence. But when water is completely still, it is in its pure, true state of transparency and reflectivity. The nature of mind is stillness, which is beyond effort. Yet the waves and ripples of conditioning obscure this truth. Emptying your mind of these conditioned habits and latent tendencies, you come face to face, so to speak, with the Tao. The Tao of the Absolute is within our natural stillness, and this natural state is where spontaneity is effortlessly born. Stillness is where the virtue of wu-wei is lived. If we come into contact with the still point of the Tao, then we begin to nourish the rest of existence through the art of living wu-wei.

LIVING THE ART OF WU-WEI

We cannot nourish the rest of existence if we are acting out of our old patterns of conditioning, and if we are trying to provide such nourishment for humanity, it will never be attained. These paradoxes are interwoven into the fabric of the universe. They often confuse us, leaving us to feel completely helpless about the correct way to act or be in this world.

Many people have a deep feeling that the world needs to be saved, but the world doesn't need to be saved. There are always two sides of a coin, something *is* and at the same time *isn't*. We are always determining right or wrong and see the good and bad side to every argument. Exploring this phenomenon deeply, we discover that everything we are discerning in the field of opposites goes according to the conditioning we have been indoctrinated with.

Our personality, then, wants to save the world, to align the world with what is pleasurable according to the personality. But the truth is that the world does *not* need to be saved, or, rather, the one who is attempting to save the world is the one whom the world needs to be saved *from*. We are trying to save the world from ourselves. Our conditioned personality conflicts with the world and with other beings because the hypnosis of one person is not the same as the hypnosis of another, so the possibility of mutual resonance in this state is nil. This leads us to complete helplessness, as all of our striving is a hindrance to our conscious growth.

This recognition of our helpless position, what Hubert Benoit called a *blind alley,* is the key that opens the door to that liberated state known in its various forms in Sanskrit as *samadhi, moksha,* and *nirvana,* and as *satori* in Japanese. This helplessness allows you to let go of all preconceived notions of how life is and how others should be. You can realize samadhi, moksha, nirvana, and satori after your personality is deflated and you realize that all your striving, struggling, and suffering are useless, because what you are seeking is already yours.

We play this mental game of striving, struggling, and suffering because this process makes us feel that we are on a path of achievement. This process of achievement abides by a linear model of reality, which has humanity running toward a goal that can never be reached. Assuming that we can achieve any goal this way is a mechanical construct. It is an attempt to control fate, while natural, nonlinear spontaneity always changes our controlled plans for life. The conditioned personality wants to enforce what it associates with pleasure upon the world by attempting to bypass the universal reality of spontaneity. Individual suffering is the result, because we are going against the grain of nature in Tao.

Suffering in life has nothing to do with nature. We suffer because our perception of reality is constantly changing, which conflicts with our rigid beliefs. We cling to a certain concrete template of life and resist change. The definite interpretation we seek in life is always changing according to our conscious growth, as the external world will mirror a different meaning to each individual's inner world. In complete helplessness, we discover that life has no categorical "right" interpretation, as all interpretation is still within the field of a linear model built on opposites. Trying to interpret life is only a way of perpetuating old patterns that need to be transformed. These patterns keep us "seeking" stillness to provide nourishment for the world, as if it were not already in our possession. Aligning with the Tao cannot be sought after, especially from a conditioned mental state. What we are really searching for can only be lived.

Our linear circuitry is a complex web of psychic phenomena that builds the illusion of a separate identity in our minds, eclipsing our nonlinear nature. Living the Tao can only be realized when this linear circuitry is brought into the order of nature. The art of living, as Lao-tzu would put it, is not a step-by-step process of unfoldment, as the linear world would suggest. Instead it is a way of living your own li, which then harmonizes with all other aspects of nature. Our natural patterns can never be realized if our conditioned patterns continue to plague our awareness. The more we cling to life, the more we continue to suffer from these patterns.

Instead of acquiring more, Lao-tzu would suggest less. We take pride in ourselves when we are armed with a lot of intellectual knowledge, yet stillness can never be lived if we have not emptied out our faculties.

Emptying the mind does not mean that we become stupid. On the contrary, we can only make use of what we have learned in life when what we have learned is not an intellectual attainment. What we learn is merely a set of tools. Problems come when we believe the tools are who we are. To unlearn, as Lao-tzu would suggest, is to not be bound by anything life has to offer. Even the idea of unlearning or emptying the mind should not be thought of as a definite route to spiritual liberation, because such states should come naturally to an individual. It is only when we reach that complete state of helplessness that a real spontaneous growth can sprout within our consciousness. When we realize that there is totally nothing to be done to recognize our true nature, we finally let go of all the limitations and deviations of the mind that held us hostage. The old regime of thinking is transmuted into a higher cognitive state of receptivity, simplicity, and humility.

Loosening the grip of conditioning sometimes requires a lot of inner strength on our part. But it is only from there that the stillness of Tao will speak to our inner ear of intuition. When we are not attached to life, life shines brightly, because our perception has been cleansed.

We believe that the external world endows us with the wisdom of the universe. Yet that concept runs against all principles and laws of nature. As an artist endows a blank canvas with paint, so do we endow the external world with life. A blank canvas remains blank until an artist endows it with what is within him. Art is not produced from without to within; it is the function of nature in the individual. Art is expressed from an individual's li from the inner world to the outer world, no matter whether it is writing, painting, music, filming, or gardening. In our modern world there are not many people who express their own natural art because their organic pattern of li is polluted with linear systems. This is why some of the greatest artists throughout history have lived lives detached from the limits of society, religion, and culture. To be deeply touched by their art is to realize that they were inspired by Tao.

Following our own li allows the Tao to enter the canvas of life. This is exactly the same as the Christian theme of "bringing Heaven to Earth." Inspiration helps others to realize their own innate potential, and, if their conditioning is not deeply rooted, they will begin to explore their own potential li. *Inspiration* means to be "in spirit," but it could also be seen as the space that enters an individual's consciousness when she is inspired. Expressions of art inspire human life and bring it back into harmony with nature.

When one follows one's natural li, the art it produces inspires the world and creates mutual resonance, ying. During this process, the formless Tao enters the world of form. Just like in nature's ecosystem, following one's own li harmonizes one with everything else in the world, generating a mutual resonance. This is the Way of *real* human nature. It contradicts linear conceptions of forcing and controlling life as a means of gain. Our natural li is only discovered when we cease our search for power.

PART 2

THE SCIENCE AND PRACTICE OF AN EFFORTLESS MIND

4

The Virtue of the Nonvirtuous

The organic pattern of li is a riddle to our conventional way of thinking. This riddle can be explored by three questions: How can we discover or be in accord with our li without being ambitious? How do we try not to try to be in the effortlessness of wu-wei? How do we become natural with no effort? From the perspective of Lao-tzu, seeking and ambition are bound to a linear model of the world, but the li that we seek out originates in the nonlinear world of spontaneity. Searching for our own li is a paradox that can tie us in knots. If you "follow your bliss," as the American mythologist Joseph Campbell suggests, how do you eradicate ambition from your mind? The little occult classic *Light on the Path* by Mabel Collins delves into ambition's paradoxical nature in its first four precepts:

1. Kill out ambition. [. . .]
2. Kill out desire of life.
3. Kill out desire of comfort.

4. Work as those work who are ambitious. Respect life as those who desire it. Be happy as those are who live for happiness.[1]

These four precepts would cause a world of confusion to a mind plagued by ignorance. But for those people who have deepened their introspection, they are essential for liberating the intellect from the hypnosis of linear continuity.

To assimilate these precepts, we need to understand how they can be perceived from two different perspectives. From one perspective, we long to create, and yet from another, absolute creativity is intrinsic to our nature and can only be accessed in the present moment. The relative version of ambition is the most common one in our world. It makes people strive incessantly for results from their creativity, as if the result were more important than the process. In this way ambition in pursuit of social success becomes insanity.

The ambition we need to "kill out," as *Light on the Path* suggests, is relative ambition, which is tied to the linear perception of past and future. This view runs in the opposite direction to Lao-tzu's and also to the Buddha's teaching that happiness is really contentment in every moment of life, while happiness in the sphere of linear ambition is only achieved momentarily, in the end result. Contentment is discovered with Collins's fourth precept: one has let go of striving for a result and instead become content with a process that is driven by one's li when ying (mutual resonance) occurs. Li, from the Taoist perspective, is an *absolute* principle that belongs to the universe. This real ambition, which we discover in our li, is the intrinsic virtue of the Tao. In the natural, nonlinear world of li, a creative process is hindered when it is planned. A true creative process and the essence of art is that your virtue can only come through your li when you have thrown off the idea of planning and striving, and instead opened yourself up to the present moment, where the natural harmony of li will grow spontaneously.

The cosmic fragrance within the universe is the virtue of the li pattern found within all organisms. Real virtue is different from the virtue of Confucian thought, as well as from the modern goal of ambition for success. Li's artistic expression is produced by a virtue that arises spontaneously, without forethought or intellectual contrivance. This virtue naturally and spontaneously dawns upon the individual when the power they seek subsides into an honest humility. This natural virtue is known in Chinese as *te* (德: Wade-Giles *te*, Pinyin *de*, see figure 4.1) and in Sanskrit as *dharma*. (In Chinese *te* can mean *power* or *virtue*, depending on how it is used. *Dharma* is an inclusive word that can mean duty, mission, law, the Buddha's teaching, and virtue. In classical texts the two terms are often used interchangeably.) The *te*, or *dharma*, of the ancients is rarely found in humanity. In many cases it is only recognized in the inspirational expressions of an artist or the wisdom of a sage. A small minority of artists and sages have access to this realm because they have naturally fallen into the nonlinear world of the present moment, where their li harmonizes with the world and inspires it as a result. The te of a sage and artist is readily available and never contrived.

VIRTUE OF TE

Te is not isolated to certain individuals; on the contrary, it is the innate cosmic nature that we all possess, as these aspects of our nature are absolute qualities of consciousness.

So if these aspects are our innate nature, why does te only come through the mind of the inspired individual? Te is as nature is; it cannot be induced or contrived, because it manifests naturally through one's experience. The answer, then, is that our motives ruin the natural unfoldment of consciousness. Our world is so hell-bent on acquiring power that we lose sight of how anything in this world is produced. When we exhibit force or seek power, the underlying motive is the instinctual impulse for survival. This tendency reinforces the illusion that we do not belong to the world.

Figure 4.1. Te—universal virtue
By Dao Stew

Our current anxiety for survival is manifest in the world through individual and social unrest, not to mention ceaseless wars that occur around the globe. The ambition that drives us toward social and material success is none other than our vain attempt to stand on the shoulders of others, as if we were somehow above others in the pecking order. These lower drives have remained in our minds from our evolution out of the animal kingdom. And the materialistic notion of "survival of the fittest" has not helped. Yet such seemingly concrete theories are slowly being torn down, because they are causing a kind of entropy in the human race. The growth of anything in nature cannot be forced, nor could there be anything to achieve from such a conquest.

In much the same way, the higher states of consciousness that lead to evolution and enlightenment are not things one can force or induce. Virtue, or te, cannot be thought of as something to acquire. This was the issue that brought about differing views between Confucius on the one hand and Lao-tzu and Chuang-tzu on the other. Confucius thought that the virtue of te was something that one could cultivate and induce, as he did not believe that it already belonged to one's own consciousness. This perspective is still aligned with a searching and striving for power, and it is diametrically opposed to Lao-tzu's.

In Lao-tzu's *Tao Te Ching,* he explains that the highest virtue is nonvirtuous, so "therefore it has virtue." And paradoxically he states, "Low virtue never frees itself from virtuousness, therefore it has no virtue." The virtue of the *Tao Te Ching* is without intellectual meaning because true virtuousness is beyond virtue. It's not something requiring thought. The te of the sage is a quality beyond the parameters of the linear world.

Trying to discover or induce the power of virtue implies that we do not possess it already. The virtue of the nonvirtuous, or te, is only available to those who do not use force or seek power. When we fervently seek power or use force, we exhaust our system by swimming against the current of life instead of flowing with it. A sage or an artist allows life to present itself instead of dictating toward life. Skillful athletes also follow this template of effortlessness.

When you finally realize, beyond intellectual speculation, that the whole universe is happening to you *right now* all at once, you will cease projecting yourself onto the world, because you will become receptive to the universe. This will align you with a real trust in life that confirms that you belong. Your li is a nonlinear pattern that organically grows out of the universe to bring harmony to the world. The li of each individual belongs to this universe, but sadly, very few discover this essence because of a world that is built on the blindness of force and power.

When a large number of the human race are not living their own li, they contribute to entropy. When te does not shine through us as individuals, we are inherently led into distractions. And we currently live in a world full of distractions, which keep our attention hypnotically away from the world within. Distractions become our sole focus, because they engage us in the sense-perceptible world with which we mistakenly identify. When we pollute the senses with external stimuli, there is no chance that the light of te can come through our minds.

ALLOWING THE LIGHT OF VIRTUE TO
SHINE THROUGH THE DARK CLOUDS OF MIND

The wisdom traditions teach us to be conscious of the nine gates of the human body. These gates are the two eyes, two ears, two nostrils, mouth, penis or vagina, and anus. They stimulate the six senses, which are smell, touch, taste, seeing, hearing, and thought. (The wisdom traditions teach that thought is the sixth sense and that it is influenced by the energy we consume through the other five senses.) The "Eye of Horus" in Egyptian symbolism, known as *wadjet* in Egyptian, is an image that contains the philosophy of the six senses (see figure 4.2).

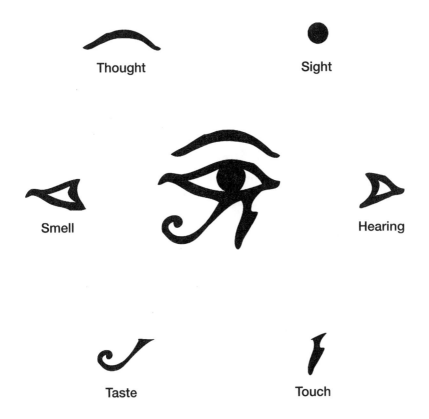

Thought

Sight

Smell

Hearing

Taste

Touch

Figure 4.2. The Eye of Horus: The Six-Sense Philosophy
By Dao Stew

When we refrain from bombarding the senses with pleasurable stimuli, the virtue of te is more likely to shine through the mind. But it is the sense of thought that, in many cases, distorts the awareness of virtue, because one has not experienced nirodha, stilling of the mind. The question, then, is, how can we sincerely attain the virtue of the nonvirtuous? Te is an absolute quality of Tao; it is omnipresent, yet in many individuals it is veiled, like the sun on a dark and stormy day.

All of the energy we consume, whether it be food, beverage, or impressions, contributes to our emotional, feeling, and thinking states. The way we receive and transform energy is continually suppressing the virtue of te, because the energy we choose for our physical and mental well-being is almost invariably toxic. From the food we eat to the liquid we drink and the impressions we allow through our eyes and ears, we are constantly poisoning ourselves through a pursuit of pleasure, as entertainment becomes more valuable than health.

According to the ancient sciences of traditional Chinese medicine (TCM) and ayurveda of India, the cleaner the fuel, the purer the thought vibrations within the mind. Even though this should be obvious, it is not, because we have divided the functions of the mind and body into separate components. But the body and mind are themselves ying: they are interdependent systems, which, when brought into harmony, allow for the spiritual plane of consciousness to come through.

The health aspect of finding one's te is really only a piece of the puzzle. The well-being of the body and mind may settle the energetic streams of the human organism, but in the majority of cases this does not clear out the *vasanas* (Sanskrit for *latent tendencies* and *habitual ways*) deep within consciousness that affect our karma (Sanskrit for *action*), and both of these continue to reinforce our *samskaras* (Sanskrit for *mental impressions* or *subliminal psychological imprints*) that bind us to the wheel of samsara, the endless cycle of suffering. This process of purifying our karma, vasanas, and samskaras is explored at length in my book *Fasting the Mind,* which focuses on the tools and framework that facilitate this complete transformation. In *Fasting the Mind* I explain this process of fundamental transformation through the relationship between karma, vasanas, and samskaras, but in brief this is the process:

To dig into our samskaras, and thus to escape the wheel of samsara, we need to work backward, beginning with karma. When we realize the dilemma we are in, we start to examine our actions, questioning our habits and tendencies. This process is achieved through the science of mind fasting (which I will discuss later in this book). Exploring our karmic actions, we need to start taking away the familiar distractions that alert us to act. We need to refrain altogether from acting toward the world for a certain amount of time.

Our samskaras begin to be transformed when we have worked through our karma and vasanas (the two limbs of the samskaras). Having stopped our usual unconscious movement of actions and habits, we arrive at the subtle sensory level, the root level of the samskaras.

These latent tendencies and habitual ways originate from the hypnotic conditioning we have undergone from birth—the samskaras. But trying to alleviate vasanas, habits, through a practice that only focuses on the conscious connections between the body and mind is an egotistical attempt to deal with a spiritual symptom. It is like a marathon runner who thinks she can sprint the whole marathon. If she attempted this, it would not be too long before she burned out her system.

This system burnout is common among many practitioners of hatha yoga, qigong, t'ai chi, and other movement methods, including forms of dance. When we try to alleviate dormant vasanas solely through the conscious movement of energy between the body and mind, we can potentially exhaust our system. We discover this among many schools of spiritual cultivation, where the pursuit of alleviating vasanas to transform samskaras usually turns into a gross exhibition of spiritual pride. Just as an athlete becomes egotistically proud of his status and achievements, so does a spiritual seeker when she sets out to use primarily the body and mind to achieve enlightenment without transcending the conditioning that drives her sense of a separate and isolated identity. As a result, her conditioned identity grows deeper roots within the samskaras, which in turn show up even more powerfully in the way she expresses herself. Think of a peacock who is strutting its stuff, and you have a clear image of what is being said here.

The health of the conscious connection and movement between the body and mind is only one aspect of allowing the virtue of the nonvirtuous te to shine bright. For the sincere student, it can be a beautiful path and practice, but it can often lead to spiritual pride and peacock consciousness as a result of its emphasis on the physical, which is a common trap of the materialist mentality.

In ancient India this connection confused people for thousands of years, as the core of the Hindu philosophy of Vedanta, known as "The Science of Self-Realization," was mainly thought of as a system of knowledge enabling one to attain a hygienic state within the physical and mental planes of consciousness. This process is incomplete, because, as many ancient wisdom traditions teach, consciousness is composed of three planes: the physical, mental, and spiritual. Many spiritual seekers in ancient times were missing the most crucial aspect for alleviating their vasanas and transforming their samskaras. That crucial aspect is the individual's awareness of and relationship with the spiritual plane.

Like many wisdom traditions, Vedanta is a framework built upon the mysterious essence of the universe, known in Sanskrit as Brahman, which is the equivalent of the Chinese Tao. Vedanta was interpreted in many different ways over the course of time, because individuals who are not centered within themselves usually create superficial systems of beliefs around the actual teachings. These systems usually pertain only to the physical and mental planes of consciousness—the world we can experience—but not to that unexplainable essence beyond experience. As a result we become connoisseurs who are eating the menu.

PATANJALI'S YOGA OF MUTUALITY

These many differing interpretations of Vedanta changed when the great Indian sage and author of *The Yoga-Sutras,* known as Patanjali, brought clarity to the wisdom that came out of the Upanishadic era. Patanjali recognized the frustration of those who could not transcend their own karma, vasanas, or samskaras. According to Patanjali, the cure for this frustration is obvious: we have overemphasized the doing aspect of life as a result of our focus on the material world. Patanjali understood that virtue will never enter an individual if the doing aspect of the physical and mental planes is the only one activated. The spiritual plane was of the utmost importance to Patanjali. He set out to devise a system of liberation that would bring the light of dharma, or te, into the world.

In the two millennia since the time of Patanjali, yoga as we know it may have changed its outward garments, but its essence is the same. When Patanjali uses the word *yoga,* he is describing a "yoking" process in alignment with its Sanskrit root *yuj,* which means union, or in Patanjali's view, absorption. His practice of yoga is intended to free consciousness from being habitually caught in a gravitational pull toward the external world. Yoga, in its purest essence, is to cease identifying with external things and instead to turn the attention inward to discover that underlying pure awareness known as *Purusha* in Sanskrit, which is the fragrance of Tao/Brahman/Tathata/Allah/God. Patanjali's classical yoga avows a strict dualism between *prakrti* (the cosmos and its movement, energy, and matter, the physical and mental planes of consciousness) and Purusha (pure awareness of the transcendental Self). Purusha, according to Patanjali, is separate from prakrti, even though the fundamental purpose of prakrti is to realize Purusha and bring its essence into the world.

Patanjali's original system, then, is not only hatha yoga (the common yoga practice that is associated with physical exercise and fitness), as the modern world mistakenly assumes. Nor is it isolated within the confines of the eight limbs of yoga (known in Sanskrit as *yama, niyama, asana, pranayama, pratyahara, dharana, dhyana,* and *samadhi*) or the seven paths and temperaments of yoga (known in Sanskrit as *mantra, tantra, karma, raja, jnana, bhakti,* and *hatha*). Patanjali brought back the archaic Vedanta system of union with the Godhead (yoga), which consists of combining a method of practice with nondoing—wu-wei. What was apparently obvious to Patanjali was that a lot of individuals are either busy practicing some form of spiritual cultivation or they are trying to remain in a contemplative state of nondoing, with both extremes ignorant of their mutuality. Patanjali understood that to practice a form of spiritual cultivation is the masculine, yang principle of the universe, and that nondoing is the feminine, yin principle of the universe. For Patanjali both practice and nondoing complement each other like husband and wife, yang and yin, Heaven and Earth, hot and cold.

Practice and nondoing are ying, interdependent, and "mutually arising." This is known in Chinese as *hsiang sheng* (相生: Wade-Giles *hsiang sheng,* Pinyin *xiangsheng;* see figure 4.3). The mutual arising of practice and nondoing is a mirror of how the universe is. From the universal perspective, consciousness and matter arise mutually. In other words, the universe produces consciousness, and consciousness evokes the universe. Both are complementary—hsiang sheng—and depend on each other—ying. According to Patanjali, it is only when we bring practice and nondoing back together that we can give birth to the spiritual plane of consciousness. The masculine and feminine function in the same way on all planes, so it would be absurd to believe the doing of

Figure 4.3. Hsiang sheng—mutual arising
By Dao Stew

practice and the art of nondoing lie outside of this cosmic principle.

Nondoing in the context of wu-wei, as we have mentioned, is the nonforcing or noncontrolling aspect of the receptive nature of the universe, the yin, feminine principle. In Patanjali's system of yoga, nondoing can be cultivated through the process of nirodha, stilling the mind. The more one sits in the quietude of stillness, the more one truly begins to live wu-wei. Stillness itself is yin. There is a resonance between being completely in the present moment of stillness, or nothingness, and the nonforcing expression of wu-wei.

It may be difficult to grasp why the more you can remain in the now of the present moment, the more you will be in the receptivity and humility of wu-wei. Nevertheless, this is the reality of our experience, as Patanjali and Lao-tzu knew. This experience is essentially the yin nourishing the yang, meaning that stillness benefits action in the same way that meditation is an advanced tool for the preservation of intellectual life. Patanjali's formula requires a sincere approach to one's own liberation, withdrawing one's focus from the world of forms, both physical and mental, into a genuine introspection within oneself, which is where the world really resides. To practice this formula, we have to be sincere in what the ancient masters call "the great work of eternity." It is only in the sincerity of the great work of eternity that we could bring the wisdom of the formless world into the world of forms, or in other words to bring Heaven to Earth.

We cannot have access to the virtue of the nonvirtuous, te, if we are continually attracted to the gravitational pull of the external world. If your attention is focused on worldly affairs, the Tao cannot make use of you, because your awareness is hypnotized to believe that the world of forms is a concrete reality.

But actually it is our perception that shapes reality, and everybody's perception of reality differs. For example, something as simple as a tree "means" something different to each and every one of us through the way we feel and interpret what a tree is. And yet how could we interpret what a tree is? This extends to anything we perceive and experience in life. It is at the heart of many conflicts between religions, because the concept of God is interpreted differently as a result of dogmatic beliefs. Many of our problems are essentially matters of belief versus belief, with no true understanding.

The Taoism of Lao-tzu and Zen Buddhism, which are two of the more mature spiritual traditions on the planet, approach the interpretation of such concepts as God in a vaguer manner, but this vagueness actually gets to the heart of the matter more precisely. For example, in Taoism and Zen, to try and give God a meaning or interpretation is like trying to write on water. The actual reality escapes the use of language and words. So the more mature approach is to know and transform your inner world while allowing the outer world to run its own course without your interference. This approach adheres to Patanjali's discovery that both the nondoing in the inner world and the individual doing of spiritual cultivation in the outer world reduce the propensity of consciousness to be pushed around by the play of form. This is what yoga truly is.

Even though many masters know that to be overly disciplined is a crutch, they are aware that spiritual discipline is necessary for those individuals who can only intellectualize the truth rather than actually feeling and experiencing it.

Practice and nondoing are necessary, because it is not until the settling of the mind, nirodha, occurs that the virtue of te will spring forth from the Tao through one's own nature, li. An old analogy is that of the sun shining through a dirty window. The more sincere one becomes in transforming and transcending one's inner conditioning, the cleaner the window becomes for the rays of the sun to shine through. The sun in this sense is the Tao, and the window is our mind.

BREAKING FREE OF THE MACHINE THROUGH VIRTUE

The virtue of Lao-tzu cannot be lived if the seals and veils of conditioning continue to obstruct the window of mind. The majority of the world's population act out of their own seals and veils, hypnotically believing that they are their conditioning. Identifying with one's conditioning is the state of the masses, and this position of rigidity, a state of sleep resembling mass hypnosis, in its turn generates an uncreative mentality and a lack of artistic virtue. Te is missing from a civilization when social, cultural, ideological, theological, and religious indoctrination is conditioned into individuals as a reality that they should abide by for their whole lives, without ever questioning its authority. The Catholic Church is a perfect example of this form of indoctrination.

Sages and artists throughout time have always questioned the authority of these institutions through their own te. They have never been concerned with opposing the machine with their own agendas, but instead their focus on te brings forth their organic pattern of li and so brings harmony to the world, regardless of the functioning of the social machine. This in turn inspires others to do the same by finding the li of their own intrinsic nature.

Te is coming from the formless realm of Tao, while the tyranny of the social, cultural, ideological, theological, and religious machine will always be limited to the incessant control of external life. Hence the machine has a use-by date, while te is limitless and eternal.

Though this is the reality of te, the masses have come to the point where they are behaving and living like machines. We are not computers or machines, but we have begun to mimic them. We remain continually disposed to being alien to this world, which only perpetuates our unnatural attraction toward the machine's tyrannical operations. They keep humanity in a paranoid state focused on survival.

We begin to break free of such hypnosis when we sincerely open our minds and hearts to an unwavering trust in life. This trust is the alchemical ingredient that brings the naturalness of Tao, te, and li together as one. The human being corresponds to nature by allowing all aspects of universal life to take their natural course without conscious interference.

This is the ultimate spiritual revelation of Lao-tzu's Taoism and the essential outcome of Patanjali's system of integrated practice and nondoing. When the cultivation of stilling the mind through nondoing has taken root in the individual, the more receptivity, humility, and wu-wei begin to reveal themselves through his or her own being. Patanjali stressed this approach because he knew that the virtue of dharma/te can only come into this world through living wu-wei truthfully. You cannot discover your own natural virtue unless you live wu-wei. In completely focusing our attention within, we bring our inner and outer worlds into order. To trust the universe means to let life *be* without trying to impose our will over it in any way.

While letting life be may mean decay or death in the cycles of nature, the human kingdom is the only aspect of nature that actively and consciously opposes the growth of life through a parasitic desire to control its own experience. We have built a model for the world to follow on the back of this parasitic desire. We are opposed in all facets of our life by an unnatural system, both within and without, that goes against our natural trust in life. Trust can only be born when we as nature are allowed to express ourselves through te. Yet the inspiration that te brings into the world is constantly opposed by the unnatural illusion of control. As we grow both individually and collectively, it is imperative that we discard all unnatural systems so that we can go past our current pattern of entropy.

5

Parasitic Patterns of the Unnatural World

It is hard to fathom the experience and life of an organism when it undergoes a cycle of entropy. From a human perspective, we see species come and go almost on a daily basis. Yet we need not be too distressed about this fact. The scientific point of view holds that all organisms will eventually decline, only to bring forth new life, because a fundamental principle of the universe is that energy can neither be created nor destroyed. According to the first law of thermodynamics, we only have transformations of energy. This law states that "energy can be transformed, i.e. changed from one form to another, but cannot be created or destroyed. It is usually formulated by stating that the change in the internal energy of a system is equal to the amount of heat supplied to the system, minus the amount of work performed by the system on its surroundings."[1]

The extinction of certain species is usually attributed to human activity. But we cannot be the sole cause of everything that goes through entropy, because this is of a universal nature. We cannot fundamentally explain the cosmic unfolding of Tao, as this is beyond human comprehension. But it would appear that whatever the intelligence of the Tao is, it knows exactly when an organism has exhausted itself and what process of transformation it should go through, like the transformation from a caterpillar into a butterfly, for example. We can never categorically know why such a transformation occurs, although it does happen in the same way that we go through our own sort of transformation at death. But we cannot comprehend what is behind that mysterious door.

ENTROPY AND DEATH? OR DEATH AND TRANSFORMATION?

Though we know that entropy and transformation are a reality, what does this mean for the human race? From our current position, we would like to think that we are outside of both entropy and transformation. But the reality is that we are blind to what this experience may be like for us in much the same way that we cannot fathom what it is like for other life forms.

The way the world is now, with all of its suffering—could this be how entropy presents itself to human life? Are famine, poverty, greed, cultural hypnosis, and wars the physical and mental advent of entropy? We all feel this suffering, and our instincts are informing us that we are undergoing some sort of process of change. But in many people the "fight or flight" tendency keeps them in fear that the beautiful human race has now begun its descending course. Though this may be the common perception of our current situation, the Way of the Tao moves in a manner that is beyond the intellectual notion of good or bad. If we could step back from such dualistic perspectives, we would discover that the human species is an astonishingly complex system, and we can determine whether it is in our best interest to move on and exist in another direction.

Our fate is the choice we make right now. And our choice becomes clear when we can step out of the analytic detail of life and discover a holistic perception of the human kingdom. From this perspective, it would be absurd to assume that the human race is going through any form of physical annihilation; rather we evolved on this planet in order to transform into something of which we cannot yet conceive. The many civilizations we have produced on Earth are nothing short of breathtaking, especially when we consider that everything we have created on Earth is driven from within the primordial place that we call Tao. Nevertheless, these cosmic vibrations continue to flow through our psyche as spontaneous thoughts that inspire the canvas of life. This cosmic flow of Tao through the human mind is increasing exponentially in the modern era, because we are undergoing the death and transformation of a different kind.

The inspiration of li, which harmonizes with the world through many individuals, comes when a monumental choice has to be made. A common trait among all organisms is that when a species is on the precipice of extinction they are somehow compelled to adapt and evolve. The human race has been residing on the precipice of extinction for quite some time, and now it is our turn to go through a death and transformation. According to many ancient cultures, we have been going through this process for thousands of years, but it is only now that we can understand that it is the inner world of the individual that drives either decay or transformation.

The choice to do sincere self-work and contribute to the great work of eternity is the small change that will transform the whole world piece by piece. We can avoid the decay of our species if we become aware on the physical, mental, and spiritual planes of consciousness. Our transformation does come at a cost, because there does have to be a death, but death does not always take the form of physical decay. Being the complex organisms that we are, death for us is different than it is for other species. The death that we are going through is taking place within the inner landscape of the individual.

In order for both the individual and the collective to transform, we need the parameters of the unnatural world to either change or die. Everything that has brought suffering to us is due to the fact that we believe in the illusion of a linear world, where we can control life to suit our own temperaments. The disharmonic aspects of suffering—famine, poverty, greed, cultural hypnosis, wars, and all forms of conditioning—can all be alleviated if we undergo the death of the linear world and come back into natural harmony. The way of the natural world is the only possible way by which any form of evolution can take place.

As I have mentioned, the natural world is a mysterious expression of a nonlinear spontaneity coming from the depths of the unknowable Tao. The unnatural world is a mental construct built on control, while the natural world is something that grows of itself. Identification with the external world alone causes the majority of humanity to project their insecurities onto the social fabric in a vain attempt to avoid responsibility for their own fears.

Our intellect discerns between pleasurable experiences and those that are viewed as unpleasant from past experience. In this fear of past experience, we discard the very thing we should embrace. When we do not embrace our fears and become responsible, these ignored emotions and feelings become tyrannical and dictatorial. The failure to look within ourselves has made for us a relationship with the world that is rigid and one-dimensional.

The institutions of our society and culture are of the same disposition as the psyche from which they arose: they are based on security and the fear of control. When we perceive only the world of forms, we wrongly assume that this world is built upon a step-by-step process with a linear structure. This is the masculine aspect of perception, which is born in the logic of the left brain. Existing and thinking in such a way leads to an unnatural concept of reality. A good example of this is how many religions erroneously believe that God is an entity bound to the human limitations of form, time, and space.

We are constantly attempting to translate our experience of reality through linear methods. But if nature is nonlinear, how could we interpret it through a linear process? This unnatural perspective on life must be exposed, both within and without, for us to grow.

CHAOS OF THE LINEAR WORLD

The unnatural world is usually thought of in the superficial sense of man-made structures versus naturally growing organisms. Yet as we have established, nature is the spontaneous receptivity of the nonlinear world as opposed to the control and planning of the linear world. When we inquire into our own lives, we discover that when we try to control or plan our experience, we invariably encounter heightened feelings of anxiety and stress. This occurs because we have overstrained our system in order to try and force the issue, whatever it may be. All of this leads to unbalanced individuals whose vital force is continually spent in trying to appease their own intellectual and social conditioning. The result is constant frustration in our lives.

In giving away our individual responsibility, we have created linear-based institutions and organizations. They are built on the premise that evolution is a straight-ahead, time-bound concept, a view that keeps humanity in a state of hypnotic servitude. Government, politics, banking, religion, and the commercial sector are all constructed on linear rules, regulations, and laws, which make all of them part of an artificial, unnatural system, centered on force, control, and the illusion of lasting success (though the spiritual core of some religions, especially Eastern religions, is based on individual liberation). These institutions are not part of nature because they are designed to control humanity, which in the end makes us feel that we do not belong.

The present-day chaos is fueled by governments, politics, banking, religions, and commerce, because these organizations embed an unnatural way of being and thinking into our psyches. As a result, a fight for control, both individually and collectively, has begun in earnest. For example, these institutions demonize death, as if death is an inherently bad thing that one should ignore and somehow avoid. This linear concept develops a fear of death that allows us to be ruled by society and culture. This is the art of government, which preys on our acquiescence. When we succumb to such systems, we shed our humanity for sheep's clothing.

HARMONY OF NONCONFORMITY

In a linear world, the external order dictates an artificial way of life to the individual, creating a conformist society and forcing us to relinquish our power to a machine that is unnatural and devoid of life. This passive conformity can be traced back to the origins of the Vedic Hindu caste system and the feudal system under medieval Western Christianity. When a settled agrarian culture such as these is born, it tends to build towns, not only to protect people from outside influences, but also to develop a mental framework based on rules and regulations.

The complexity of agrarian culture leads to a division of labor and a division of function. From this division, the ancient Hindus (the Vedic civilization of Dravidians and Aryans) developed a caste system. The Hindu caste system is made up of the Brahmins (priesthood), Kshatriyas (nobility), Vaishyas (merchants and farmers), and the Shudras (laborers). A direct parallel to the Hindu caste system can be found in medieval Christian society, where we see the priesthood and the church, feudal lords and nobility, farmers and merchants of the commons, and the serfs.

Although we no longer have a caste system, this underlying pattern is still with us today. When we are born into this world, we come out of our mother's womb (nature) and are taught to submit to the rules of society and culture according to our socioeconomic status. This is the crucifixion of the individual; it is the sacrifice we all make. According to the tyranny of the machine, this crucifixion is for the "common good" or "greater good." But there is a stark difference between the Hindu and Christian societies of ancient times.

First of all, the function of the Vedic caste system was an act of surrender to Brahman (ultimate reality/godhead). Individuals would crucify their egos and their desires in favor of the lives they had been given by nature. This means they would not seek another path or to try and control their lives according to their interests. Instead they would abide by the order of society, which helped them diminish their egos so that they could feel the presence of Brahman within themselves. This is dharma as social duty. The second difference is that, once Hindus have fulfilled their social duties in this life, they are allowed to break away from caste and become renunciate sages in the forest, a practice and title known as *vanaprastha* in Sanskrit. (This possibility is loathed by Christian society, because one is thought of as useless if one does not contribute to the social order.) This breakaway from caste is viewed as a return back to nature and could be thought of as a resurrection. A sage is not part of society and does not conform to its rule. Jesus was a sage in this mold. This is why he was not thought of as a particularly good member of society and he was actually put to death (if we take the story of Jesus to be real). Those who submit invariably lose their natural innocence. Conformity is the result of force. When individuals are forced by society and culture into life situations that are against their will, they give away their natural sovereignty in exchange for comfort and servitude and are psychologically reduced to sheep. We have developed this sheeplike behavior as a result of the belief that the morals and ethics forced upon us by society are avenues to success and freedom. But this notion is absurd inasmuch as the success and freedom of our world are unnatural. These goals are gauged only by finances. But obviously this is not true success or freedom, as money is empty and void of meaning, and it provides no happiness other than that of acquisition. Happiness cannot be contained in anything that we need to force to happen.

As human life is forced into a sheeplike way of being, happiness is reduced to momentary stimulants of excitement. In such a life we can never express our natural divinity, li, because we are following the model of someone else's idea of life. Yet conforming to anything other than one's own innate world destroys us physically, mentally, and spiritually, as te, the virtue of Tao, cannot come through the organic pattern of the individual, li. Anxiety, depression, and stress are so prevalent in this day and age partly because we are forced to live such lives. Wars and social unrest then reflect the individual's anxiety.

Liberated individuals are in alignment with their own nature and with the Tao. They do not benefit the accepted social order and are regarded as useless in the eyes of institutional and organizational power. Lao-tzu and Chuang-tzu were treated this way, because they could see the unnaturalness of an artificial society. The Buddha and Jesus of Nazareth were two other such sages who could see through the hypnotic veil. A liberated sage understands that anyone who continues to act out the unnatural patterns of conditioning is contributing to chaos and destruction, either consciously or unconsciously. One who is liberated, on the other hand, begins the yoking process until a crystal-clear perception of the Tao in reality can be experienced. In Richard Wilhelm's translation of the *I Ching,* he states:

> Not every man has an obligation to mingle in the affairs of the world. There are some who are developed to such a degree that they are justified in letting the world go its own way and in refusing to enter public life with a view of reforming it. But this does not imply a right to remain idle or to sit back and merely criticize. Such withdrawal is justified only when we strive to realize in ourselves

the higher aims of mankind. For although the sage remains distant from the turmoil of daily life, he creates incomparable human values for the future.[2]

Evidence for these "incomparable human values" can be found in the legacy that a sage leaves behind. Lao-tzu is a good example. It has been over 2,500 years since he lived, and yet his wisdom still reverberates within our consciousness today. This is the power of te.

As I have mentioned, the virtue of te is only available to those who do not seek power, control, or force. Governments, politics, banking, religions, and commerce, on the other hand, are constantly striving for control by forcing the population to their will. This poses a significant hurdle for humanity to overcome. What would it take to bring the individual and the collective back into harmony with the Tao? How can the natural course of the Tao grow unfettered from these parasitic patterns?

6

Natural Government
Born of Tao

Some of the greatest leaps for humankind will be taken when we face the dire dilemma that binds us to a mechanistic world. Drastic measures are needed to reorient our awareness back toward the natural world of the cosmic unfolding. From a sage's perspective, the answer to humanity's plight is not, how do we rid ourselves of these unnatural systems, but instead, how radical are we willing to be?

Taoist teaching emphasizes that if we understand the spontaneous function and unfolding of the universe (Tao), then we will not fight this process; if we live effortlessly, with wu-wei, the natural harmony of the cosmos will prevail.

We cannot eradicate the established governmental apparatus by governing more. This was one of the major differences between Confucianism and Taoism: Confucian ideology built a strict system whereby one should govern one's life both within and without in accord with its philosophy. Lao-tzu, on the other hand, would have deemed this perspective absurd, because the fundamental aspects of any external form of governance—control, force, and a search for power—actually put one out of sync with the natural harmony of the universe. As a result, we feel as if we do not belong here.

To govern is to control, and control is built from the experiences of the past and a plan for the future. Nature in all its glory is locked out, which is why a different system of government cannot be the way out for us. If we can be sincere in living wu-wei, we will allow the course of Tao to run its path back into harmony through our own nonaction in regard to the dilemma at hand. Revolutions and protests do not change anything, because they are still reacting out of human conditioning and seeking to control life. To govern is to control, to control is to destroy life, and this is what needs to be reversed through the way of nature and wu-wei.

Human beings have the intelligence to comprehend the nature of wu-wei. Yet many people do not have the knowledge of wu-wei naturally, through their experience, unlike all other organisms, which would seem to jeopardize our claim to being the most intelligent species on this planet.

THE NATURALNESS OF TZU-JAN

To seek refuge from these unnatural systems, we need to understand nature itself. The organic pattern of the individual (li) is our innate nature driven by te, virtue. Nature, then, has no relationship to force, control, or power. The order and pattern of nature is not a forced order, as nature is not bound by external influence or control. The Taoist term for *nature* is the Chinese *tzu-jan* (自然: Wade-Giles *tzu-jan*, Pinyin *ziran*, see figure 6.1), which means that which is spontaneously of itself. When a natural organism is in harmony with all life, it grows of itself spontaneously. Tzu-jan can only arise of itself without external compulsion.

Tzu-jan is the essence of the yoking process found within the spiri-

Figure 6.1. Tzu-jan—nature spontaneously of itself; naturalness
By Dao Stew

tual core of many religions, and especially in the origins of Chinese and Indian wisdom. When we withdraw from our conditioned perception of reality, we come back into nature and grow spontaneously in harmony with all other components of life. What would happen if we let go of control? When we leave the animal, plant, and mineral kingdoms alone, they continue to grow and prosper without any interference. What would happen, then, if we left people alone?

From the perspective of traditional Taoism, if we left people alone to follow their own passions and interests, harmony would prevail within community, no matter how large or small. If there were no interference from the external world, people would follow their natures, because passive obedience would no longer be a way of life. We would no longer feel the need to obey unnatural organizational patterns, because in following our own nature we would begin to harmonize with other people and the environment. When we leave life alone, Tao runs its natural course, and all aspects of life come into order without seeking order.

Superficially, this perspective may be incorrectly perceived as "anarchy." But there is a major difference: anarchists' motives are driven by what they oppose. On the other hand, the sages who understand tzujan just follow their own nature without any concern for institutional or organizational power, because they are content to let such things run their course. An anarchist is still distracted by external influences. So if the world is thrown into anarchy, then the motive destroys the project. Nature *is* as it *is* and can have no motive, nor is it a project to embark upon. Tao can never be induced, as its principle happens spontaneously of itself—tzu-jan. Anarchy is an attempt to induce Tao so as to bring about a real order through an intellectual, artificial decision to abandon the ways of society.

NATURE'S ANARCHY

Though anarchy in some sense is a step in the right direction, it is not a suitable method for liberating the world, because it cannot avoid having an agenda. The Russian evolutionary theorist Peter Kropotkin understood this subtle difference between anarchy and tzu-jan. Kropotkin postulated that if we were to leave people alone to follow their own nature, a real social order and true government would emerge out of the current system. His theory is almost a carbon copy of the Taoist tzu-jan; its depth is equal to the thought of a sage. Yet his political theory was called anarchism (labeled Kropotkin's Anarchy) so that many people could conveniently put it in a superficial context and believe they understood it.

As radical as Kropotkin's theory may appear, it is this trust in people's nature that will bring about a true, harmonious government out of the ashes of a dying culture. This is in alignment with Lao-tzu's wisdom. The true government, according to the Taoist perspective, is the communal power that we attain when we trust one another sincerely to live our own lives without interference. This is the te of the collective, or we could say social virtue, because true government is only realized when we have given up the power to govern. In giving away our power, we gain the sort of power that we truly want, which is beyond control. In the same way that we give our power of virtue away to get a real virtue beyond virtue, we give our power to govern away in order to get a real government beyond government. Life is governed when we leave the world alone to be what it will be. This is the paradox of life, although it confuses our linear, logical view.

In the classical Taoist text left behind by Chuang-tzu, known simply as the *Chuang-Tzu,* he profoundly articulates this teaching:

> I have heard of letting the world be, of leaving it alone; I have never heard of governing the world. You let it be for fear of corrupting the inborn nature of the world; you leave it alone for fear of distracting the Virtue of the world. If the nature of the world is not corrupted, if the Virtue of the world is not distracted, why should there be any governing of the world?
>
> Long ago, when the sage Yao governed the world, he made the world bright and gleeful; men delighted in their nature, and there was no calmness anywhere. When the tyrant Chieh governed the world, he made the world weary and vexed; men found bitterness in their nature and there was no contentment anywhere. To lack calmness, to lack contentment is to go against Virtue, and there has never been anyone in the world who could go against Virtue and survive for long.[1]

In going against our nature, tzu-jan, we not only destroy ourselves but we also contribute to the annihilation of the human race. The government we have created out of our insecurity and irresponsibility has to come to an end, or we as a species will succumb to the fate that all parasites experience. The big question we need to ask is, how do we take steps to sincerely trust others and let them live life as they choose? If we can leave people alone, then the world will naturally heal its wounds and begin to grow in harmony with the Tao. But none of this is possible if we have not confirmed the reality of tzu-jan within our own being.

Even though the wisdom of wu-wei and tzu-jan have existed since the time of Lao-tzu, there has always been only a small minority who are sincere in bringing peace into their hearts and the hearts of others. Most humans, on the other hand, resemble a leader of a nation who parades around proclaiming peace through forcing war upon the world.

Such insanity exists because individuals' versions of peace are built on their own agendas and attuned to their conditioning, which is incorrectly identified as pleasure. Many people will not admit this, because they are still identified with the seals and veils of conditioning. In such a state, we are like a tree that is continually pruned to grow straight and rigid. But our nature can never be straight and rigid, because we are eternally connected to the Tao, which is beyond name and form. Even the hypnotic feeling of straightness and rigidity arises out of the Tao, although temporarily, like a wave in an ocean.

TRUST IN PEOPLE IS REAL GOVERNMENT

We can only leave people alone to live their own lives if we are sincere in our own introspection and willing to discard the conditioning that clouds our unity with our brothers and sisters. When we are sincerely humble and free from agendas, we nourish and secretly transform the world—again, through *not* seeking to transform it. A sage has no agenda, and this brings spiritual oxygen into the world. We all have undergone various sorts of conditioning and we all have the same physical and emotional states, so we can sympathize with the rest of the world, which suffers as a result of the same hypnosis as ours. On the other hand, if we are all inherently the same, we also possess the same qualities that a sage lives by.

The *I Ching* (see figure 6.2) demonstrates through a complex system of sixty-four hexagrams how a small piece of the puzzle can transform the whole system when that small piece allows for change, which puts it back in accord with the Tao. This is to be thought of psychologically. The change in the small piece wears away the edges of its rigid hardness and softens its nature, which is a metaphor for a human allowing the ever-changing universe to soften his rigid conditioning into humility. When this process takes place, tzu-jan, nature, and virtue, te, bring the light of Heaven, *tian* (天: Wade-Giles *t'ien*, Pinyin *tian*) in Chinese, into the world through the uniqueness of an

Figure 6.2. The eight trigrams that build the sixty-four hexagrams of the *I Ching*
By Jason Gregory

individual's li, organic pattern. The *I Ching* incorporates Taoist principles to intellectually and spiritually verify the reality that a single drop of water in an ocean causes a ripple effect, especially when that droplet is purely reflective and transparent. Tzu-jan is a predominant principle in the *I Ching*. For example, when a small piece begins to grow spontaneously of itself, it will have an effect on the whole system, which in time will compel the whole to follow suit.

All of Taoism is built upon this concept of natural growth, which brings one into accord with the Tao and as a result affects the whole. In observing nature, sages such as Lao-tzu discovered that every organic system grows out of another system whose current state no longer serves its position in life. This is the natural process of growth, death, and rebirth. The organic world does not discard the old but instead grows slowly out of the old into a new state. The organic world builds upon old, because everything in life serves its purpose. Anarchism does not follow this pattern: its method is to oppose the status quo with its own agenda for bringing order to the world.

Contrary to this method is the Way of Lao-tzu, which follows the reality of the natural world. Tzu-jan is exactly the way nature is, and human beings are that as well. When we have retreated from external compulsion, we grow spontaneously as nature does and in turn we affect the whole. We are slowly growing out of civilization in its current state, even though the majority of people are not conscious of this change. The paradox here is that if we continue to fight our current system, no natural change can happen, as we still do not trust in the situation at hand.

For organic life to grow out of the old and into the new, it has to accept the conditions it has been dealt and begin to resonate on a higher level in order to build upon the lower. Our current social and cultural systems have served their purpose. Nevertheless, they are no longer needed, as our lessons have been learned. Problems arise in the growth of our species when we believe that the past was a mistake. This again reveals a hypnotic sense of not belonging. Real trust acknowledges that everything we have gone through, both individually and collectively, is exactly how it was supposed to be. No matter how much senseless bloodshed has occurred on this planet, it has gotten us to where we are now and could have been no other way, because where we are now is exactly where we need to be. Life is always fundamentally *right,* but we have to get out of concepts of good and bad to realize this. We have to have an inclusive view of reality rather than the exclusive view we are accustomed to.

Tzu-jan can only come to fruition when we trust that everything the universe has produced is fundamentally right and could be no other way. The systems of government, politics, banking, religion, and commerce are unnatural, but they have gotten us to a certain point, and we have learned many lessons from them. It is just that they are no longer needed. The true government of the *real world* will grow out of the sickness of the old to heal the world from its hypnosis.

If we cannot trust the world and the people in it, we stand no chance for survival, because a species at war with itself is doomed. You, the individual, can begin the process, but it really depends on how sincere your trust is. People often say that they trust the universe, but then they consistently condemn life according to their conditioned perspectives. If we are to assimilate wu-wei, we need to be radical enough to let life go its own way. This will allow us to be seeds of growth, which will change the world without our intention to do so.

7

Trust Is Unity

Sincere introspection will reveal aspects of your inner and outer worlds that you do not completely trust. People belonging to dogmatic religions often say that they trust God, and that God is love and God is one. But when we observe these people, they are in many cases judging other people or other religions as if this "one God" had made a mistake. Hence there is a lack of trust in their narrow concept of God. The spiritually mature, however, can see how the lack of trust imbedded into our consciousness serves as a blockage to the light of God, or in the terminology of Taoism, the Way of the Tao.

In our speech, thoughts, and mannerisms, we exhibit a propensity to doubt life. We usually doubt that we can achieve anything, so we continue to cling to our own conditioning. We doubt because we have been taught that we are alien to this world and that somehow we do not belong. This fuels the mind's bias toward negativity. The deluded mind always seeks to change the circumstances of life to suit its own conditioned perspective. Conversation takes on a negative tone. When we are positive, we are not doubting, because sincere positivity is an affirmation of life. Yet in a world that feels cut off from life, we think of positivity as a disgustingly strange attitude.

The trust we have lost is the result of the deluded, unnatural world in which we find ourselves. But we should not get too distracted by this fact, because to assume that any of this was a mistake is to move away from trust. Again, we are growing out of the old and into a new way of life, which at the moment is beyond our comprehension. At the same time, if we do not comprehend the trust of wu-wei and see how it is a universal reality, we may fall back into old patterns. And paradoxically, if this were to be the case, we would need to trust the unfoldment of that process as well. This unwavering trust does seem unattainable to the deluded mind. But when you sink into the depth of your own being, you will know that this is the only reality, and that any other type of reality would be absurd.

TRUST IN LIFE

Even though to trust yourself and life is the only sane way to experience this world, most of us do not understand the practicality of this way of being and its value for true freedom. Many people are swept up in the doing aspect of life, so they seek to change the world. But this approach—to only *do* and never allow life to take its own course—confuses them deeply. Not only do they lack trust, but their doing comes out of their conditioning.

But if our motive for doing anything comes out of our conditioning, how could the unity of humanity prevail on Earth? To separate yourself from humanity by acting out of your limited beliefs only harms the world. It is not an act of peace but a subtle act of violence. Indian philosopher and spiritual teacher Jiddu Krishnamurti poignantly articulates this violent separation of beliefs:

When you call yourself an Indian or a Muslim or a Christian or a European, or anything else, you are being violent. Do you see why it is violent? Because you are separating yourself from the rest of mankind. When you separate yourself by belief, by nationality, by tradition, it breeds violence. So a man who is seeking to understand violence does not belong to any country, to any religion, to any political party or partial system; he is concerned with the total understanding of mankind.[1]

The practical value of a trust in life, yourself, and others should be self-evident, but our intentions, no matter how good, are, again, plagued by conditioning. Wars are a testament to this fact. Wars are invariably waged because of the delusory belief that humanity is divided by the boundaries of nations and religions.

Even though the practical use of trust can be comprehended intellectually, it is only when we live by it in our own lives that we can understand that freedom is the result of trust, or in other words, wu-wei. As we are the microcosm of the world, any process and any knowing that can be verified within us is also a reality in the world as a whole. We contain the complete picture. True freedom at the heart of this picture is beyond our beliefs and conditioning. This is known when an individual is sincere in her own introspection.

The Tao can only make use of you when you are empty of all that blocks a union between yourself and the universe. The unity we seek is not an intellectual understanding, but instead it is a *sense* of unity. Yet unity, and a sense of unity, exist only in a liberated mind, which is the authentic contribution that one can make to the possibility of a unified humanity.

The root and essence of both consciousness and the universe is that everything is connected and ultimately one. The universe in its awe-inspiring totality produces consciousness, and consciousness evokes the universe. Both are inseparable and paradoxically the same. The big picture and the small picture are one.

A sage knows this intrinsically, because the mind, when emptied of all its hypnosis, begins to replicate the eternal space of the universe, showing that the foundation of consciousness is space. Yet this should not be misunderstood. The essence of consciousness is not a blank state, as many spiritual seekers believe. On the contrary, while consciousness is exactly like space in emptiness and vastness, it is also like space in that it contains the whole universe. Consciousness, like space, is always open to new experiences and change. The liberated mind functions in this way, leading to trust. In the same way that consciousness evokes the universe, so does trust evoke a sense of oneness in the individual. The truth and reality of the universe and consciousness are one, but trust is where the oneness is realized within our being.

UNITY, TRUST, AND WU-WEI

When you trust the universe, you become one with it. Wu-wei dawns upon the individual in the same way, because when we let go of control, we gain the indescribable power and virtue of Tao. This relation of trust and oneness is the principle of living wu-wei. When you are humble enough to leave things alone, you begin to feel a sense of unity intuitively. Lao-tzu's words in the *Tao Te Ching* reveal this trust for the individual whose inner ear is attuned to the rhythmic silence of the Tao. The wisdom of Lao-tzu was not to intellectualize oneness, but instead to feel it and know it.

Organized religions teach the individual about the unity of life only intellectually, because any dogma is in its essence separate and isolated. So the teachings of these religions reflect this isolation, as they assume that we are separate from God. Nevertheless, the core principle of all religions is to find God within yourself. This was the template of the *philosophia perennis* (perennial philosophy). The saints and sages of our past explained that in finding God within, you understand how oneness is the only reality. Thus the Latin *religare* (the root of the word *religion*) and the Sanskrit *yuj* (the root of the word *yoga*) are both words that describe the union with God that can only be found within. Yet this does not mean withdrawing from the external world, because this unity within us is what brings unity to the world. The spirit of one's unique li brings harmony to the entire world as the tool, so to speak, of the indescribable Tao. Once our conditioning is out of the way of Tao, the peace residing deep within us knows nothing other than trust, because that is the acknowledgment of unity.

It is the *feeling* of oneness that we really seek—a feeling of oneness within ourselves that is never disturbed by the fluctuations of life in the outside world. When we are disturbed, we lose sight of our innate love. We never truly love the world in this way, because we condemn it on the basis of our own conditioning. The only way to truly love the world is to trust it with a trust that cannot be moved by the deluded mind. Trust is the validation that the universe is one and that you do belong.

We have built doctrine after doctrine in trying to explain the universe and our relationship to it. But these attempts are intellectual pursuits rather than a direct experience of unity. In our overemphasis on the intellect, we have lost sight of the beauty of life, which stands beyond reason. Religion attempts to intellectualize God, philosophy attempts to intellectualize the universe, psychology attempts to intellectualize the mind, and with all this we destroy the world in trying to give it meaning for our puny intellects. *God, universe,* and *mind* are all conceptual. Yet they are referring to the transcendent, that which is beyond time and space (although it includes time and space). The problem in our world is that we get stuck to the intellectual meaning. From this we build our idea of the world, which exists only in the realm of names and form. This state of perception discounts the inner world; as a result, our planet is in a constant war among peoples of supposedly different nations, religions, races, and genders. These catastrophic results stem from the fact that our explanations always come from a separatist point of view. How could we explain such things as God, the universe, or the mind from a conditioned perspective?

We are constantly attempting to measure the immeasurable. It is impossible to explain categorically why trust opens the feeling of oneness within. Being the mere humans that we are, there are just some things that we can never explain, and this is precisely the point of self-realization. We can't intellectually explain why trust is the way of unity, but we can confirm this in our own experience. If we were sincere in living wu-wei, we would understand the truth of unity through our trust in life taking its own course.

It is impossible to explain the Tao, trust, and oneness in Taoist wisdom. It is very much like the Buddhist doctrine of the Four Invisibles. Alan Watts states in *The Way of Zen:*

> The Buddhist doctrine of the "Four Invisibles" is that the Void (*sunya*) is to a Buddha as water to a fish, air to a man, and the nature of things to the deluded—beyond conception.
>
> It should be obvious that what we are, most substantially and fundamentally, will never be a distinct object of knowledge. Whatever we can know—life and death, light and darkness, solid and empty—will be the relative aspects of something as inconceivable as the color of space. Awakening is not to know what this reality is.[2]

Intellectually knowing about trust and oneness misses the essence of the experience, because these two are both dissected as relative aspects of an absolute reality. The union with the Tao is only known as a living reality when the so-called relative aspects have dissolved into their original oneness. The sense of unity that we seek to discover can never be something that we could theorize or speculate upon. As

I have mentioned, the very use of language itself is isolated to the field of duality, so all the investigations of religion, philosophy, and science are futile if they ignore consciousness in giving preference to intellectual study.

The Eastern wisdom traditions, especially Taoism and Zen Buddhism, seek to eradicate any such intellectual debate or speculation, because they know that a trust in self and life leads to the unexplainable peace of oneness. A Chinese Zen master of the ninth century CE, Tung-shan Shou-ch'u, was once asked, "What is the Buddha?" and he spontaneously answered, "Three pounds of flax." Many philosophical debates have been hatched about the meaning of this reply but fall short of the mark. From the Zen perspective, Tung-shan was bringing the questioner into the reality of the *now moment*. The irrational answer of "three pounds of flax" extinguishes any idea of intellectual theorizing and speculation, which is the sole purpose of any great Zen *koan* (*koan* is a Japanese word for a problem or riddle that admits no logical solution). A koan is a story, dialogue, statement, and ultimately a riddle, which is used in Zen practice to provoke great doubt in the student's mind as a way of testing his progress. One of the oldest koans can be found in the *Chuang-tzu* text, and this is why some scholars believe Zen Buddhism is a tradition built in part on Chuang-tzu's wisdom. In this passage he uses complete nonsense to puzzle our intellectual faculties so that we stand back in awe and are brought back to the ground of the irrational impartiality of life:

> There is a beginning. There is a not yet beginning to be a beginning. There is a not yet beginning to be a not yet beginning to be a beginning. There is being. There is nonbeing. There is a not yet beginning to be nonbeing. There is a not yet beginning to be a not yet beginning to be nonbeing. Suddenly there is nonbeing.[3]

Wow! Trying to make sense of such a passage is impossible—and that's precisely the point. Actually, Chuang-tzu is using humor in this passage, because even in his day people tried to use logic to understand the meaning of the universe and our existence, only to arrive at erroneous conclusions.

Koans are famously employed by Zen masters to throw disciples back into the present moment, where process has no beginning or end because thinking has completely succumbed to the irrational.

One such encounter with a koan is described in a story in which a disciple was summoned to the Zen master's home. The master told the disciple that he wanted an exhibition of Zen tomorrow. Leaving the master's quarters, the disciple was confused about how he could put together such an exhibition. That whole night he tossed and turned in bed, anxious about how to please the master. The next day, on the way to the master's home, the disciple was still fretting about the problem when he saw a frog that is unique to Japan. "Aha!" he thought, and he took the frog to the master's house. When he arrived, the master asked, "So can you exhibit Zen to me?" In reply, the disciple showed him the frog. The master gave a slight smirk and said, "No, too intellectual." In other words, his exhibition was too contrived, too well thought out. The very thinking about it thwarted the project. To answer the master somewhat authentically in this regard requires no thinking, as Zen is the natural spontaneity of the universe in the eternal now. So to exhibit Zen is not to worry about it, because Zen is life.

When we try to give a logical, intellectual explanation to such a reality as trust, we lose sight of its significance in our own experience. Many masters past and present, such as Tung-shan Shou-ch'u and Chuang-tzu, have had no time for philosophical debate about the reality of Tao. They would rather give you a direct experience of it so you can taste it for yourself.

When we step outside of all the learning we cling to, we come back into that sense of unity. It is the individual's choice whether or not to live wu-wei, as this depends on no external source. To retreat from external compulsion is a gesture in favor of trust, because no outside source of learning can take away your innate connection to the universe. The peace that resides in the unity of trust allows the individual to harmonize with the world. This not only brings the light of Tao into the world but also guides and helps the individual along their journey through life. When we trust, the universe answers us through the resonance of our experience. The feeling of oneness brings the individual back into accord with the function of the universe, like a child nourished by its mother's bosom.

TRUST, AND THE UNIVERSE IS YOUR BODY

When we trust completely, our physical, mental, and spiritual planes of consciousness harmonize with the heartbeat of the Earth. When we have cleared the passage for Tao to function through us with its natural velocity, the rhythms of our bodily functions and vibrations of our mental states move as an extension of the Earth.

A perfect example of this complete trust and harmony with the planet is the *Kon-Tiki* expedition of Norwegian ethnographer and adventurer Thor Heyerdahl in 1947. In this amazing story Heyerdahl and his crew drifted on a balsa-wood raft from Peru out into the vastness of the Pacific Ocean. From a logical perspective, this attempt to just drift into the vastness of the Pacific would appear suicidal. But somehow, in true Taoist wisdom, Heyerdahl had a trust that his own organism and the ecosystem of the Pacific would harmonize together as one if they were given the time to do so.

Without exercising the use of force, Heyerdahl's trust that he and the ocean were a unified system allowed the power of te to manifest.

As he and his crew drifted into the unknown, the balsa wood of the raft began to swell up and bind the logs together more securely, which gave their raft the durability to take on the tough conditions of the Pacific Ocean. The issue of food was another obstacle to overcome. Yet astonishingly, as a result of their complete trust, flying fish were on their deck every morning.

Rejecting the fear of the unknown, Heyerdahl and his crew began to replicate the intelligence of dolphins, because they were in perfect harmony with the course of nature by following the path of least resistance. The trust in following the path of least resistance is the power of te, which is a reflection of how the power of lightning follows the path of least resistance and also of how the Tao works through an empty mind. A full mind is resistant. In the *Kon-Tiki* adventure, Heyerdahl's trust was answered by what we would deem miraculous events. Yet from the wisdom of sages like Lao-tzu, these events would make perfect sense, because our organism is an intrinsic part of nature. Astonishingly, as Heyerdahl continued to follow the ocean's natural rhythms, he and his crew drifted 8,000 kilometers (5,000 miles) from Peru all the way to the distant islands of the Tuamotus of French Polynesia in the South Pacific.

Heyerdahl's trust made him an aperture through which the universe could express its nature. His trust, though it may appear extreme, was the feeling of unity he had within by living wu-wei sincerely. In denying the use of force, Heyerdahl demonstrates how the power of te can change the world without any intention of doing so. When we oppose our own experience and try to control life, we develop an unnecessary anxiety within ourselves, because we fear the uncertainty of the future. We attempt to dictate to the future through our plans, and though these plans may be good in theory, they are in reality phantoms and distractions from the unity that can be found in trust.

Thor Heyerdahl is an example of what each and every one of us can live by if we are radical enough to throw off our fears of the past and future and instead live completely in the here and now. Our intentions to change the world are the result of humanity separating itself from the here and now. But it is only when we can be completely present in the here and now that we will know what is best for the future. Trust and unity arise in the crystalline clarity of stillness. Our movement out of this state tends to make us suspicious of the world. As a result, we fall into the average state of mind, which is constantly rearranging the pieces of the puzzle to try and somehow make sense of the world according to its conditioning.

All of our intentions to change the world are fundamentally flawed, because the very intention to change the world implies that we do not trust the world. The unnatural systems of government and politics are built on this lack of trust. Their primary intention is to change the world according to their agenda.

Government and politics are erroneously thought of as instruments to bring unity to the world, but the very essence of both is designed on the premise of a world divided. Anarchy and revolution are also flawed, because they arise from the idea of opposing the status quo with yet another agenda of changing the world. This perception of the world, which we have all adopted, is a step in the wrong direction. We believe that we need to work toward unity, yet our intentions are plagued by ours and others' conditioned isolation. How could we work toward a unity that is already innate in our nature? The unity we seek is already there, but it is only revealed when we trust the world.

Changing the world in the hope of discovering unity is like a knife trying to cut itself. How can we search for something that is already there? Unity can only come from trust. Thor Heyerdahl had no intention to reach any particular destination; thus he reached where he was meant to go with no forethought or preplanning. His trust was his strength, and the guidance that led him on his journey was his union with the universe responding to his basic needs.

In any attempt to change the world, we destroy the world, because the very intention to change something is built on the illusion of separation. Organized religion is a good example of this process, because many religions make people feel separate from God. In feeling separate from God, we are taught that we should pray. But the very act of prayer is, to a degree, a lack of trust in God. When we pray, no matter how morally elevated our prayers may be, we are trying to force God's hand in order to satisfy our conditioning and pleasures (unless the prayer is in selfless gratitude to the All). We arrogantly try to deny the destiny that is mapped out for us through praying that nothing unpleasant happens to us. To force God to your will in prayer is to lack trust in God. We are trying to change the world's circumstances according to our own beliefs and preferences.

We will never experience the harmony with all life that Thor Heyerdahl felt if we continue to exhibit a lack of trust in any part of life. Trust and oneness are verified when we completely let go of ourselves and let the Way of the Tao guide our life. But this guidance can never come if you are anxious to change the world or force God's hand. Our intentions for life and ourselves are the very motive that distorts the future. Attempting to force God's hand with prayer is the same as trying to change the world, because both acts destroy the world. But the world destroyed in the act of praying is the world within yourself, as you incorrectly assume that you are alien to this universe.

Trust and unity come to those who do not experience the world with the filters of conditioning in their minds. Peace on Earth can prevail if we can individually follow our own paths in life with no resistance to the unfoldment of the Tao, which will surely soften our hearts. It is when we force our lives to be a certain way that we are blind to where the Tao is guiding us. The language of the Tao can only be known when all operations of force have ceased within the psyche. The true power of te, virtue, comes into its own when control and force have ceased within our minds. The trust that abides within us, though it is often veiled by our conditioning, is what will allow the naturalness of the Tao to unfold on our planet. But if we are not attuned to that trust, we will not be able to read the signs leading us to our fate.

8

The Practice of Yin Cultivation and the Art of the Skillful Craftsman

Lao-tzu's Taoism led to the unfolding of sciences to understand how the entire universe is our body. The essential premise of these ancient Taoist sciences is how our psychosomatic organism aligns and comes into harmony with the formless realm of the Tao and with the movements of the heavens. As I mentioned, no external form of governance can bring this about, because the fundamental principle of external government is control and force. What is required to achieve harmony with the Tao is a heightened level of self-governance. This level is attained by understanding your mind and body more deeply, which allows you to understand the greater universe more intimately.

It is possible for any of us to achieve the miraculous feats of Thor Heyerdahl, but we have to understand how the macrocosm and microcosm are one and how that union is only achieved from abidance in trust. Yang Zhu's discovery of the body, which I briefly mentioned in the introduction, eventually led to the Taoist sciences and practices of martial arts and traditional Chinese medicine (TCM). Both of these sciences are an extension of Lao-tzu's *Tao Te Ching*. They extend his philosophy into a science with practical application for daily life.

But modern-day students and practitioners of martial arts and TCM lose sight of this fact. These misinterpretations have been growing for thousands of years and are at their peak now. It is the result of interpreting Eastern philosophy through Western and New Age filters and also of the growing population of modern Easterners who have lost contact with their traditional roots. (All these and the problem of taking metaphors literally lead to a misunderstanding of key concepts, which then leads to an unintelligent spirituality.) This leads to our modern cultural habit of embracing control, force, and intellect at the expense of wu-wei. Essentially this means that our world embraces the yang (masculine/Heaven/active/doing/heat) over the yin (feminine/ Earth/passive/nondoing/cool), which is slowly but surely destroying the world.

THE SKILL OF MARTIAL ARTS IS
YIN OVER YANG

The science and practice of martial arts are based to some degree on the science of TCM. This is evident in the fact that TCM focuses on how our body is a miniature inner universe. When we know and understand this inner universe, we begin to know the greater, outer universe and see how both function the same. Martial arts make use of this idea through movement methods that are supposed to open up the meridian channels of the body. This allows qi to flow freely, so that the mind and body are in harmony with the effortlessness of the heavens. This experiential knowledge attained by martial artists is supposed to transfer over into daily life, as it did with Thor Heyerdahl.

Trust, then, is at the heart of martial arts, as they are based on the fundamental Taoist philosophy of wu-wei. The problem with martial arts is, as I have mentioned, that they have been infected with the cultural tendency toward doing, which becomes an intellectual game of striving for a so-called goal. Our whole world is invested in the energy of yang at the expense of yin.

Our modern habits of doing, control, and force are deeply entrenched in both spiritually oriented and combat-oriented martial arts. And yet the core of both methods is the same, as martial arts are about transforming your character to reveal your true nature. This is the spiritual heart of martial arts, but it has been misinterpreted by Westerners and also by numerous people in the East. Many people think that the spiritual transformation in martial arts is about attaining powers or experiencing some altered state of consciousness similar to a psychedelic experience. This way of thinking is the "amateur spirituality" to which Chuang-tzu alluded. Amateur spirituality is the attraction to peacock consciousness, meaning that people still have the yang habit of showing off or telling other people about how peaceful and lucid their state of mind is. The irony of peacock consciousness is you find these people always talking about themselves, to the point where the listener feels ill and exhausted. This is especially true for those people trying to attain supernatural powers, called *siddhis* in Sanskrit.

Such proclamations prove that no real transformation has occurred. All that has occurred is that one has become a well-trained show pony. This show-pony attitude is yang oriented and has nothing to do with the basis of martial arts. As a result martial arts in the modern world are based on the perpetual activity of yang and failing to embrace the nondoing of yin. We discover this yang-over-yin temperament in the sport of mixed martial arts (MMA), which is best-known through the organization of the Ultimate Fighting Championship (UFC). The athletes of MMA are well-trained; many of them function at a rate of peak performance, which can be quite a spectacle to watch. But the problem is that many mixed martial artists and spectators believe martial arts are about talking trash and beating the hell out of the opponent. Though this may be entertaining for the spectator, we should not delude ourselves into thinking this has anything to do with martial arts. Rather it is just martial arts on steroids, polluted with the idea of yang over yin, doing over nondoing.

This attitude inclines one toward competition because of its innate characteristics of force and control. If mixed martial artists, or any combat sport athletes, for that matter, were serious about martial arts, they would need to understand and embrace the essential tenet of cooperation. Cooperation in martial arts is evident in the internal practice of pushing hands, known as *tui shou* in Chinese. In the practice of pushing hands, each person is feeling and moving according to the energy of the opposing person. Pushing hands works to undo our natural instinct to resist force with force by teaching the body to yield to force and redirect it. Force does not exist in this practice, because in feeling and moving according to the energy of the other person, we are accessing our receptive yin nature. Yin evokes the art of cooperation. Although it may appear that pushing hands is a form of competition, it instead is a dance, as you essentially need two to tango. Even so, pushing hands, like many other aspects of martial arts, has succumbed to the tendency toward the yang characteristics of competition and peacock consciousness.

In both spiritually oriented and combat-oriented martial arts and MMA, the yin art of cooperation is at the core of all forms of cultivation. For example, if a mixed martial artist is trained properly, he or she will know that there is no opponent other than himself or herself. You are essentially testing yourself against your so-called opponent. The only opponent is yourself, and your perceived opponent is a mirror of where you are in your training. The mirror of the opponent reflects back to you your spiritual development as well as aspects of your character that have not been transformed or cleansed out of your psyche. So no matter what form of martial arts we are talking about—including MMA—the essential heart of the art is to blunt your sharpness.

Blunting the sharpness is a phrase used by Lao-tzu in the *Tao Te Ching* to describe the softening of one's rigid personality. In martial arts, it is about evoking the yin qualities of humility, compassion, forgiveness, respect, and honor. For thousands of years, martial arts have been mistakenly seen as practices to cultivate the yang, masculine characteristics of power, force, and control. This incorrect perspective has only increased our tendencies toward competition and trying to stand out in the crowd. Martial arts are not based on yang over yin but on yin over yang. They are a practice that mimics life, as the majority of the time we are in the yin of nondoing. When those brief moments of time come for us to act, we are precise and our timing is impeccable.

The nature of our psychosomatic organism is to reside in yin and only activate yang when needed. This is actually the fundamental function of our psyche. Our attempts to reverse this order are causing psychological problems and mental-health issues that contribute to a world gone insane. The natural function of residing in the feminine yin while moderately accessing the masculine yang was explained by Lao-tzu in the *Tao Te Ching* thousands of years ago:

> *Know the male,*
> *yet keep to the female:*
> *receive the world in your arms.*
> *If you receive the world,*
> *the Tao will never leave you*
> *and you will be like a little child.*[1]

In the humility of yin we do not seek to be special or to attain superpowers. We go about our life quietly and do not make a noise about the mystery of Tao that we experience within our consciousness, because it is in itself indescribable. This is the elite spirituality of Chuang-tzu. This means we *know* experientially, but it is not intellectually explainable. The experience of Tao/Brahman/Godhead within is beyond knowing logically or finding a conclusion, because it is nonlinear and eternal. Only in the finite realm of existence can we come to logical conclusions and dissect with our intellect. The principal method of the practice of koans in Zen Buddhism is to overcome the intellect, and this is the prevailing philosophy of the East. In the *Tao Te Ching* Lao-tzu states:

> *The tao that can be told*
> *is not the eternal Tao.*
> *The name that can be named*
> *is not the eternal Name.*
>
> *The unnamable is the eternally real.*
> *Naming is the origin*
> *of all particular things.*[2]

This wisdom is also found in India in the ancient text of the *Kena Upanishad* from the Vedic era of India:

> *Brahman is unknown to those who know It, and*
> *is known to those who do not know It at all.*[3]

The meaning of this verse is that those who say they know Brahman still have a concept or object of knowledge in their mind. Since Brahman transcends the mind and our thinking, no concept can capture it, and so we cannot say we really know it. The academics and intellectuals who believe they can explain the universe and its mystery by somehow coming to logical conclusions are deluded. They have lost their intrinsic sense of awe and cannot witness beauty without analyzing it.

Many people in the world are in the yang habit of using their intellect as a scalpel to dissect life into pieces so as to analyze the details. Many of us who underwent a formal education had the chance in science class to dissect an animal, usually a frog or toad. When we dissect a frog, it becomes a mess. When our dissection is finished, though we can describe the frog's internal organs, we have lost sight of its beauty. In dissecting the frog, we pulled it apart into discrete pieces, destroying its inclusive totality. When we dissect life, we destroy it. This is occurring right now, as our world is embracing yang over yin, which is against nature's way.

A YIN-DEFICIENT WORLD

The perspective of yang over yin is promoted in our world from the earliest stages of education into adult working life. This perspective becomes so entrenched in our minds that we exhibit it in our ordinary life as well. We begin to anxiously think that we "should" always be doing something. We are made to believe that if we are not doing something, then we are useless and a nuisance to society. This train of thought is supported by the societal mantra "Time is money," which actually means you had better get moving or you will miss your opportunity to succeed in life. Thinking in this way gives us the illusory belief that we can control every aspect of our lives and become masters of time. Many entrepreneurs have this mindset, and though there is a skill to becoming independently successful, there are also a lot of pitfalls.

We all suffer from these pitfalls when we overemphasize the yang "time is money" attitude. They include anxiety and stress. Though we should all be creatively productive and use this life well, we have to face the fact that we can never truly control life or master time. The whole world has gotten itself into a big rush because we believe the contrary is possible. But this attitude is destroying the world, because what truly nourishes the world is being ignored—the feminine, yin bosom of the universe. As I mentioned, the fundamental function of life and our human organism is to reside mainly in the yin while activating the yang only conservatively.

In embracing only the incessant activity of yang, we are becoming a species that is out of balance and essentially sick, which is affecting all other life on this planet. The clinical diagnosis in TCM for the human race is that it is yin-deficient. In a yin-deficient world we are internally consumed by heat, because we are constantly seeking action, overthinking, and seeking distraction. Yang is the internal heat that is evoked by incessant activity, and yin is the cool of deep rest, relaxation, and nondoing that nourishes all aspects of our mind and body, and which preserves yang. The American Chinese medical doctor Brendan Kelly explains in his work that a yin-deficient humanity contributes to external climate change, because the excessive heat in our internal climate is projected into our external culture.[4]

What we are within becomes our culture. The propensity to always be doing something is a response of heat within, which becomes the heat in the external world. Excessive heat within our organism causes the heightened sense of anxiety and stress that a lot of people feel today and have even become accustomed to. This comes from being overactive, but it also comes from the yang-laced stimulants we ingest, which cause internal heat and ultimately irritation. Coffee, for example, has no real value for us; it is a super-yang bean that causes extreme levels of anxiety, stress, and jitteriness. Coffee intoxication enhances our tendency toward activity, and this in turn slowly but surely depletes our psychosomatic organism and in turn harms the planet.

To have an organism that is incessantly doing requires a lot of external stimulation, be that either heat-infused food or entertainment. As I have mentioned, in TCM the little picture and big picture are the same picture. So any change within the internal system of the human organism will be reflected in the planetary organism. If we constantly consume coffee, refined sugar, refined flour, and frivolous entertainment, to name just a few things, we will be constantly distracted and as a result will seek more distractions. Ultimately this weighs heavily on the resources of the planet and also destroys the mind. In allowing ourselves no time to rest, relax, or to just be bored, we are destroying our inner and outer world, because we are incessantly in motion and essentially overheated. What happens to any vehicle that is overheated and does not offset this with the required amount of coolant? Engine failure and a complete breakdown is the result, which is usually irreversible. This is what is happening to humanity and the planet. It is up to each of us as individuals to address our yin deficiency. We cannot go on like this for too much longer.

Wu-wei is required to heal our yin deficiency, because it is an aspect of yin. To heal our yin deficiency does not mean we stop being active, though this may be healing and helpful in the beginning. To truly heal, we are trying to find balance. Reestablishing balance requires us to come back in accord with the nondoing, forceless, and effortless mind of wu-wei. This balance of life involves predominantly residing in the yin and conservatively accessing the yang, which, as I've mentioned, is the art of martial arts.

Balance between yin and yang, then, is not about equal shares but rather natural harmony. I often use a chocolate milkshake as an analogy to describe this natural balance. For example, if we were to put 1 cup of milk and 1 cup of cacao powder in a blender we would make a mess that would be unhealthy and sickening to drink. But if we just put enough cacao powder, often a few teaspoons, for the same amount of milk, then we will have a delicious chocolate milkshake. Yang is the cacao powder, and yin is the milk, which is from the feminine bosom of life.

When we transfer this understanding of balance to martial arts, we discover a practice that requires discipline but should not overreach its limits. Many martial artists tend to overdiscipline themselves. They never alter their routines, and in a lot of cases they add more to their daily practice. This is the yang habit—the more we do, the more we will gain. This is against Lao-tzu's philosophy of "less is more." The "time is money" mantra has affected martial arts, transforming them into a predominantly yang activity with a depletion of yin. As a result, many martial artists develop rigid, overdisciplined personalities. They fear to change their habits and routines, which puts them out of sync with the ever-changing Tao. As a result they essentially become prisoners to their discipline.

The martial arts were built on the function and harmony of life, yin over yang, as yin is where the true source of power resides. When we overreach in martial arts from excessive yang we are usually thrown to the ground and defeated. In the highly eclectic Korean martial art Hapkido (extremely similar to the Japanese Aikido), when your opponent overreaches, you only need to feel her energy and movement, which requires no effort. As a result your opponent will fall to the ground without any force or effort on your part. It is the art of avoiding resistance. Residing in yin, you move with your opponent's movement, which is often full of yang force. Though you may absorb the blow somewhat, you don't feel it, because you are the pivot of balance between yin and yang in their perpetual dance. Hapkido is focused on yin cultivation. In fact, all martial arts are designed to cultivate yin, but we are often seduced by the power and force we attain from yang.

CULTIVATING YIN

When my brother-in-law Sangue Yoon was a young boy, he practiced Hapkido regularly. He often complained to his sister (my wife) and his parents that all he was learning was how to fall. He was frustrated because he wanted to learn how to throw. This is a common response for anybody who begins to practice Hapkido or for that matter a number of martial arts and spiritual practices. Learning how to fall and how to absorb and move with a blow appears pointless to a world built on the habit of force. As a result, we cannot understand the significance of learning not to be active, and this produces frustration.

A world deficient in yin has no idea how to cultivate it. Often our attempts are laced with yang and only contribute to more deficiency. This is common with martial artists who are attracted only to the yang aspect of the craft. Anyone who is overdisciplined in any craft will have a rigid mind. This rigid mind often has trouble flowing in conversations and listening deeply to the other person without the yang habit of waiting for their turn to speak (usually about oneself). You feel this distinct tension in this kind of person, not so much in their posture but in their eyes and speech. There is a distinct stiffness in their words that results from being too disciplined. This overuses the analytical mind (the PFC); this mind is stiff. Even the positivity of such people has a stench of fakeness to it. For example, when an overdisciplined, rigid mind speaks, the individual often displays an attitude implying that she is "cool" with everything, even though the other person can sense that she is pretending. Pretending to be OK with everything is a yang habit. It is the analytical intellect assuming that if we practice some form of spiritual cultivation, then we should be good and moral people who are incapable of harming an ant. We should essentially be Goody Two-Shoes.

This is an incorrect perspective because, again, we are dissecting the world into parts that are exclusively good and bad rather than following the natural inclusivity of nature. We are often possessed with the idea of *who I should be* rather than *who I am*. We overdiscipline ourselves to attain who we should be, but this idea is based on social beliefs. To try and reach this destination is an endless journey to nowhere, because it is driven by the yang of the external world. We cannot just be actively doing, doing, doing, in the hope that we will become better people. In fact, we deplete our system with this attitude, which in turn contributes to the destruction of the world.

Cultivating yin requires us to refrain from our yang tendency to always act and to overstimulate our organism. We need to apply my chocolate milkshake analogy if we are to survive. We need to learn how to fall as my brother-in-law did, so to speak. As with my chocolate milkshake, nature resides predominantly in yin. Physically and psychologically we do as well, because we are intrinsic expressions of nature. We need to learn how to truly relax—and I don't mean sitting in front of a digital device with popcorn, which in actual fact is not resting your mind.

Overdiscipline and overwork puts us at risk of system failure, which presents itself as a host of mental health issues, stress, and anxiety. As I've mentioned, being in the nondoing wu-wei of yin actually preserves intellectual life. Essayist and cartoonist Tim Kreider explains how this insight made him better at his job:

> Idleness is not just a vacation, an indulgence or a vice; it is as indispensable to the brain as vitamin D is to the body, and deprived of it we suffer a mental affliction as disfiguring as rickets [. . .] it is, paradoxically, necessary to getting any work done.[5]

Drastic times call for drastic measures, and the best method for cultivating yin is drastic but essential for our well-being. It involves fasting the mind, which I explore in depth in my book *Fasting the Mind*. Essentially it is a practice for starving the mind of any stimulation, external or internal. Methods of fasting the mind are common in the East. Two methods are found in Buddhism; they are known as *vipassana* and open awareness meditation. Vipassana meditation means insight into one's true nature. One form of practice is a strict ten-day silent retreat, which involves complete silence, many hours of sitting meditation, and a vegetarian diet for the entire period. Vipassana meditation often advocates focusing on the sensations within our psychosomatic organism, which takes our awareness deeper and has the potential to purify the mind.

Open awareness, on the other hand, is an objectless meditation in which we engage with a simple, stable posture while trying to empty the mind through focusing on the breath or by fixing the attention on something in the environment.

Advaita Vedanta, a science, philosophy, and spiritual practice originating in the Upanishads and the Vedas, offers a method of fasting the mind whereby we remain in a practice of self-inquiry by focusing on the question "Who am I?" All three methods have a positive effect on mental concentration, reaction time, motor skills, and sensory sensitivity.

Fasting the mind, though, involves more than just these three methods. It is a lifestyle that transforms life from yang-dominant to yin-dominant. This approach is nothing new. The phrase "fasting the mind" is first found in the *Chuang-tzu* text, though its practice is much older. It appears in a story about how to change a corrupt ruler. In the story Confucius is the mouthpiece of Chuang-tzu. He has a disciple named Yen Hui. Yen Hui has heard of a ruler in the Chinese state of Wei who is treating the common people very poorly. Hui has numerous plans to change the ruler, but all of them are shot down by Confucius on the grounds that Yen Hui is intentionally trying to change the ruler according to his own will. In the end Confucius has had enough and tells Yen Hui that he should fast his mind:

> Confucius said, "Goodness, how could that do? You have too many policies and plans and you haven't seen what is needed. You will probably get off without incurring any blame, yes. But that will be as far as it goes. How do you think you can actually convert him? You are still making the mind your teacher!"
>
> Yen Hui said, "I have nothing more to offer. May I ask the proper way?"

"You must fast!" said Confucius. "I will tell you what that means. Do you think it is easy to do anything while you have [a mind]? If you do, Bright Heaven will not sanction you."

Yen Hui said, "My family is poor. I haven't drunk wine or eaten any strong foods for several months. So can I be considered as having fasted?"

"That is the fasting one does before a sacrifice, not the fasting of the mind."

"May I ask what the fasting of the mind is?"

Confucius said, "Make your will one! Don't listen with your ears, listen with your mind. No, don't listen with your mind, but listen with your spirit. Listening stops with the ears, the mind stops with recognition, but spirit is empty and waits on all things. The Way gathers in emptiness alone. Emptiness is the fasting of the mind."

Yen Hui said, "Before I heard this, I was certain that I was Hui. But now that I have heard it, there is no more Hui. Can this be called emptiness?"

"That's all there is to it," said Confucius. "Now I will tell you. You may go and play in his bird cage, but never be moved by fame. If he listens, then sing; if not, keep still. Have no gate, no opening, but make oneness your house and live with what cannot be avoided. Then you will be close to success."[6]

Fasting the mind thus cultivates yin to bring about lasting balance. It requires us to starve the mind of all external and internal distractions. When we do so, we begin to affect the mind and body at the deep level of the nervous system. There is essentially a war going on in our nervous system from the overuse of yang "doing" at the expense of yin "nondoing."

The nervous system is the part of an animal's body that coordinates its voluntary and involuntary actions and also transmits signals to and from different parts of its body. In vertebrate species, such as human beings, the nervous system contains two parts, the central nervous system (CNS) and the peripheral nervous system (PNS). The central nervous system contains the brain and spinal cord, while the peripheral nervous system consists of mainly nerves, which are enclosed bundles of long fibers, and axons, which are long, slender projections of nerve cells that conduct electrical impulses away from the neuron's cell body. These nerves and axons connect the CNS to every other part of the body.

The PNS is in turn divided into the somatic nervous system (SoNS) and the autonomic nervous system (ANS). The ANS is our central focus when we are doing psychological or spiritual inner work and transformation. It is a control system that largely acts unconsciously and regulates bodily functions such as heart rate, respiratory rate, digestion, pupillary response, urination, and sexual arousal. The ANS in its turn has two branches, the sympathetic nervous system (SNS) and the parasympathetic nervous system (PSNS). The SNS is sometimes considered the "fight or flight" system because in emergencies it is activated to mobilize energy. It is what we activate when we are in motion and are being stimulated through our senses. Without it we could not do anything. The PSNS, on the other hand, is activated when we are in a relaxed state. We activate it when we essentially do nothing. The PSNS is also responsible for stimulation of "rest and digest" and "feed and breed" activities that occur when the body is at rest, especially after eating, including sexual arousal, lacrimation (tears), salivation, urination, digestion, and defecation. The PSNS is what makes us drift off to sleep every night. It is stimulated most when we relax deeply.

The war in our nervous system is essentially the overstimulation of the SNS along with an understimulation of the PSNS. When we stimulate only the former without activating the latter, we increase the probability of chemical imbalances in our brain.

Cultivating yin activates the PSNS, leading to equanimity. Fasting the mind, then, not only transforms and heals the individual but also our culture. Cultivating the cool of yin in the mind and body reduces the yang heat of our world piece by piece. It is not an overnight phenomenon, but rather a gradual process. You realize how addicted you are to distraction, and you understand that it will take time to heal it through fasting the mind. It is the same long and arduous process for the collective.

Cultivating yin and fasting the mind are both essential for understanding the effortless mind of wu-wei, which is enlightened consciousness. Yin cultivation methods affect our nervous system at the root level. In cultivating yin, we diminish the yang effects of intellectual discernment, thinking, and active doing. Diminishing yang effects also weakens the sense of "I" as a separate person. We tend to think of ourselves as an "I" in the mind, separate from our body, and many of our philosophies and religions reflect this perspective. The sense of the mind-body dualistic split is overcome when the "I" is decreased, leading to an integration of hot and cold cognition where the mind is embodied and the body is mindful.

The idea of the "I" as a ruler of the body is a notion going back to Plato's analogy, in his *Phaedrus,* of the charioteer and his wild horses that need to be tamed. Plato's charioteer is a metaphor for our mind as master (cold cognition), while the wild horses represent the untamed, animalistic, and ultimately unconscious body, but at the same time the natural and spontaneous movements of life (hot cognition). The person you think of as yourself (the charioteer), with all these beliefs, desires, and attachments, is only your cold cognition in conflict with the hot cognitive processes, which appear unconscious and untamed when they are not disciplined. This overemphasizes the mind-body split and makes us believe that this is the way a human being is in a yang-oriented world.

We experience embodied cognition, on the other hand, when our psychosomatic organism has reached a state of homeostasis, with perfect balance between yin and yang. When we cultivate yin, the sense of "I" submerges into the hot cognitive process of the body, which evokes *intelligent spontaneity*. This intelligent spontaneity is the skill of the craftsman and the art of wu-wei. The irony with skill, though, is that the cold cognition is required to process the information of any particular skill through intellectual understanding and constant repetition before it becomes ingrained in the hot cognition, becoming second nature. The skill and art of intelligent spontaneity is the consciousness of one who is in the zone.

Being in the zone occurs when we cultivate yin. Accomplished athletes, writers, actors and actresses, artists, and other achievers are adept at cultivating yin in their lives. The master of any craft has embodied his skill to such a heightened state that his actions are essentially effortless and are devoid of thought or even of a sense of a person doing the actions. The embodied skill of a craftsman, where cold and hot cognition have merged to evoke universal intelligence, is a metaphor for the enlightened and effortless mind of wu-wei. This understanding is captured in the story of Cook Ting (also known as Butcher Ding) in the *Chuang-tzu* text. In the story Cook Ting is cutting up an ox for Lord Wen-hui. Lord Wen-hui is extremely impressed by Cook Ting's skill at cutting up oxen so effortlessly. Cook Ting explains that he encounters the ox with his spirit and this allows the spiritual energy of the Tao to take over. He states:

> What I care about is the Way, which goes beyond skill. When I first began cutting up oxen, all I could see was the ox itself. After three years I no longer saw the whole ox. And now—now I go at it by spirit and don't look with my eyes. Perception and understanding have come to a stop and spirit moves where it wants. I go along with the natural makeup, strike the big hollows, guide the knife through the big openings, and follow things as they are. So I never touch the smallest ligament or tendon, much less a main joint.[7]

In China, Cook Ting's embodied skill and intelligent spontaneity is known as "seeing from spirit." Seeing from spirit occurs when the sense of "I" has diminished, which essentially means that the cold cognition has decreased its influence so that we can perceive reality from the holistic hot cognition. The Cook Ting passage illustrates how intelligent spontaneity is evoked and realized as our nature when the sense of "someone" "doing" something has disappeared. Even when life is in motion and actions appear to be happening, they are effortless, because the sense of "I" doing it has disappeared. Thus the nondoing of wu-wei evokes effortless action, where the mind is not attached or stuck to any aspect of reality.

Cook Ting's effortlessness and unstuck mind is a metaphor for the effortless mind in wu-wei *all* the time, which is the enlightened state of a sage. This essentially means that our natural state is to be in the zone all the time, but it has been eclipsed by our intellectual training, which, with its tendency to dissect life, eclipses this reality. The Cook Ting story underscores the fact that when we are in intelligent spontaneity, we are harmonizing with the environment. The cook's skill demonstrates that, when we cultivate yin, evoking intelligent spontaneity, we see that the apparent duality of an inner world isolated from an outer world is an illusion. In the effortless state of intelligent spontaneity, both realities are one and the same. But this perception can only be achieved when yin cultivation has transformed the mind into the natural effortless state.

The effect of intelligent spontaneity occurs because yin cultivation methods bring us in touch with a function of our nervous system that has been suppressed from overdoing the yang. In activating our PSNS through yin cultivation, we get in touch and become more intimate with the enteric nervous system (ENS) located in the gut.

The ENS is a meshlike network of neurons that governs the function of the gastrointestinal system. It is more commonly known as "gut instincts." Our gut instincts come from the enteric nervous system, and we can tune into them by downregulating the sense of "I." If we do, we will hear messages from the gut louder and more clearly, and we can act in accord with spontaneous reactions and judgment calls. We begin to move as though we can sense the future that we are about to experience. But all that has really happened is that the ENS is functioning without the hindrance of the prefrontal cortex and, like Cook Ting, is aligned with the environment.

Activating the ENS evokes our natural spontaneity, removing the fog of intellectual discernment. When we cultivate yin, our gut instincts are in sync with the environment and with each situation. This allows us to be natural and effortlessly spontaneous, which are signs of mental authenticity and a pure heart.

Lao-tzu's teaching of sticking to the yin with a conservative application of yang aligns you with the universal order of Tao. Your entire being becomes an extension of the universe, as the universe has become your entire body. Its magic and splendor come to life as your perception is cleansed and intelligent spontaneity has been evoked, bringing universal harmony to the world through your consciousness. When our being aligns with the universe and its process through intelligent spontaneity, we begin to experience synchronicity without needing to rationalize the experience. This process takes our intellectual discernment from merely seeing coincidence to perceiving synchronicity.

PART 3

THE ART OF
EFFORTLESS LIVING

9

Synchronicity Is the Language of the Effortless Mind

In the logical sphere built around our culture and society, we see the unfolding of life as a matter of mere chance, with no real significance or meaning. This view of ourselves as strangers to this world puts us in a constant battle with the events of life. The art of wu-wei, on the other hand, is an affirmation of life, because wu-wei is a trust in the function of the universe and how it expresses itself through human beings. Chance has no place in this context, because all events are perceived as fate and therefore have deep meaning for us. Sri Ramana Maharshi, the great sage of the twentieth century, expressed his view of the differences between chance and fate in a short note he wrote to his mother, who was pleading with him to break his practice of silence and return home:

The ordainer controls the fate of souls in accordance with their *prarabdha karma* [the karma of past experiences and lives predetermined and manifested in one's present body/incarnation, *prarabdha* is often translated as destiny]. Whatever is destined not to happen will not happen, try as you may. Whatever is destined to happen will happen, do what you may to prevent it. This is certain. The best course, therefore, is to remain silent.[1]

The silence of Sri Ramana Maharshi is the verification that he lived the power of wu-wei. Like Lao-tzu, Ramana Maharshi understood that oneness and unity are only revealed through absolute trust. When we unquestionably trust that there is a path that is guiding our life, it is complemented by a deep inner voice that we hear as our intuition. This phenomenon is commonly known as "divine guidance" or "the voice of God," even though both these terms have been deprived of their true meaning by organized religion. Leaving things alone through trust aligns your life with fate.

CHANCE OR FATE?

Chance, on the other hand, arises out of our primal instincts for survival, because we incorrectly believe we are opposed by the events of life. The idea of chance, then, relates to the unnatural, linear perspective on life. This perspective sees the future as having no significance to the way we are in the present or in the past.

Taoist wisdom rejects the idea of chance, because it is a one-dimensional perspective. Being bound to the world of form, chance excludes the inner world. Fate, which takes into account the relationship between our inner and outer worlds, is diametrically opposed to chance. This relationship is of the same essence as the natural, nonlinear world. Fate is nonlinear because it depends on our inner world synchronizing with the external world. This synchronization relates to the deep content and conditioning of our mind, which remains unconscious. The Swiss psychiatrist Carl Jung discovered this connection between the unconscious and the material world through his own experience. Jung states, "When an inner situation is not made conscious, it appears outside as fate."[2]

Jung postulates that the unconscious and fate conspire against the conscious self to further the growth of the individual. This is one of the main principles for understanding the shadow element of the psyche, as the world we experience will continue to reveal suppressed and unconscious aspects of our minds. Both fate and the unconscious uproot our plans to control life.

Our identity, or ego, is the aspect of ourselves that attempts to control and plan our present and future experience. But as we all know, no matter how hard you try to control life, it somehow has a way of changing those plans. And yet upon self-reflection, you discover that these unexpected events helped to shape your life and allowed it further inner growth. So what we think disturbs our life is actually fate and our unconscious conspiring against our rigid personality for the purpose of our evolution as individuals. As the softness of water slowly wears away at the hardness of rock, so too does fate wear away at the rigidity of our conditioned identity.

Fate relates to the unconscious—those deep aspects of ourselves that need to be made conscious for us to grow. This process has nothing to do with the ego, because the ego is built on conditioned beliefs and thinks it knows what is best for you. But your ego does not know what is best for you. It is the lazy, distracted aspect of your mind, which believes it is special. What is best for you arises out of fate, which brings to light those aspects of yourself that your ego has suppressed. Being built into the fabric of consciousness, we cannot live exactly how we want according to our identity, because everyone's life would resemble their pleasures and fantasies, and this would put them grossly out of sync with the homeostasis of the planet. This is not freedom.

In the modern era we are audaciously attempting to build a world based on our pleasures and fantasies. But we are slowly learning that nothing can be learned from a world whose chief motive is to avoid pain. You only have to look into your own life to understand that pain has humbled you and has given you the greatest growth.

This striving for control and pleasure is the major difference between organized religion and Lao-tzu's Taoist understanding of fate. The faith of many religions is based on the hope that one day the events of life will turn in favor of our conditioning and pleasures, instead of understanding that to trust fate is to have faith in God.

The Taoism of Lao-tzu says trust and fate are a single thing. Living wu-wei brings trust into harmony with fate, not because events coincide with your individual desires, but because you have let go of these desires. We are out of sync with fate when we plan and strategize about the future; furthermore, we are wasting our time and energy, because these dreams in many cases never come true. Not that it is useless to have imagination—there is nothing wrong with imagination—but the problem occurs when our imagination is linked to our personal agendas, which in turn are based on our conditioning. Imagination in a lot of cases consists of nothing more than dreams of controlling our destiny. This ultimately hurts us, as these dreams are invariably very distant from reality.

These misunderstandings distort the principal truths handed down from the mystics of each religion. Having faith that is separate from fate leads to idiotic dogmas, such as that the individual and God are separate from each other, or that God is not found in the natural world, or that this world is somehow a construct coming from God as if God were an architect and we were mere pawns in a stage show. Faith as seen by many organized religions has no relationship to the external world, because they think of the material world as something we should conquer or try to escape.

The usual notion of causality is the result of such misguided views. Many religions teach that in this world we are opposed by a meaningless cause-and-effect process, which is constantly uprooting our wishes and desires. The answer to this problem is supposedly to have more faith. Yet if the unconscious and fate are connected, could we say that what plays out as cause and effect has a deeper meaning than we may think? The *I Ching* suggests that all events in life are connected in a way that is beyond intellectual comprehension. In writing about the *I Ching* Jung states:

> This assumption involves a certain curious principle that I have termed synchronicity, a concept that formulates a point of view diametrically opposed to that of causality. Since the latter is a merely statistical truth and not absolute, it is a sort of working hypothesis of how events evolve one out of another, whereas synchronicity takes the coincidence of events in space and time as meaning something more than mere chance, namely, a peculiar interdependence of objective events among themselves as well as with the subjective (psychic) states of the observer or observers.[3]

The *I Ching* explains that all aspects of life have a deeper meaning because of synchronicity, which we experience both collectively and individually. When we trust the unfolding of fate in our lives, we become aware of synchronicity. Synchronicity is the language the Tao uses to offer its miraculous guidance. But the spiritually blind see this guidance merely as coincidence.

Wu-wei, if sincerely understood and followed, harmonizes our inner world with the outer world. This harmony is evident through the synchronicities we experience in our lives. Instead of the idea that fate is against us, synchronicity demonstrates that fate is a teacher that softens our hearts into an honest humility. If we can truly live wu-wei, the magic and miracles of the universe come to life through synchronicity. It is as if the source of Tao is speaking to us directly.

When you trust the workings of the universe, its evolutionary unfolding begins to be mirrored in your own experience. It is as if reality is guiding you and revealing a story about yourself and your place within the cosmic spectrum. Though religions speak of divine intervention, many ignore the fact that this intervention is the by-product of synchronicity. In any event, the idea of divine intervention points out a contradiction in religious belief: If God is separate from the external world, then how could He/She/It intervene in this world?

The Taoist view of the underlying source within all life should not be identified with the Western concept of an immanent, pantheistic God. This view would reduce the mystery of the Tao to intellectual jargon. Furthermore, the Taoist perspective does not see causation in the Western way, whereby each event is separate and stuck together with other separate events. On the contrary, no events can be connected, because connection in this sense would still imply separation. So the Taoists perceive the universe as one single event, with differing fluctuations in the unified field of Tao, in the way that a wave is distinct from the ocean, but it is still the ocean.

Similarly, the Taoist perspective should not be confused with the pantheistic view of the universe as a mass of distinct things and events working in an unconscious fashion. Taoist wisdom is not saying that the universe is unconscious. It is saying that abiding in what we perceive as the unconsciousness of the universe is an intelligence beyond intellectual speculation. To believe that Tao is just an unconscious energy is as absurd as the notion of a personal God ruling separate from the universe. Becoming aware of synchronicity demonstrates that there is more to the Way of the Tao than meets the eye.

A trust in life and an alignment with synchronicity affirm life on all levels, physical, mental, and spiritual. These metaphysical, psychological, and spiritual profundities are too vast and deep for the average materialist to comprehend. (Average materialists include most members of organized religions, because they are predominantly materialist in thinking and character.) The spiritual adepts of antiquity never thought of the material world as gross matter, because upon deep contemplation nature has a story to tell for those who have come to a place of nirodha, stillness, within themselves.

Synchronicity proves that the material world is not mere gross matter but the unconscious intelligence of the Tao playing out through our own being. All forms of matter, whether of a human body or a rock, have the same intelligence within them at different degrees of magnitude. The intelligence of Tao synchronizes with the external world when one follows wu-wei. This trust harmonizes both the inner and outer world through the language of synchronicity. Lao-tzu, like practically all sages, revered nature. In contemplating the interconnectedness of nature, the sages have discovered how we fit into and indeed belong to nature. Those who dwell only in the material world have no such spiritual vision. They do not see how everything is interconnected and unfolding into something that at the moment is beyond human comprehension. Many religions are based on the assumption that the world is merely gross matter and that spirit exists only in humans and not in anything else. Those who reside in pure awareness will know that this is absurd.

SYNCHRONICITY IS THE SONG OF SPIRIT AND MATTER

If divine intervention and synchronicity exist, spirit and matter cannot be separate. Sincere contemplation of nature brings this unity of spirit and matter to the forefront of our awareness. This understanding is not found only in Lao-tzu's Taoism, but it is common in the East and at the very core of many spiritual traditions. The spiritual science at the basis of Gnosticism and Hermeticism esoterically explains how spirit and matter can be one. The Hermetic tradition, as set out in a book called *The Kybalion,* explains in seven laws how spirit and matter, or in other words the inner and outer worlds, are in mutual relationship to each other. The laws of vibration and rhythm show how spirit and matter are in a constant dance, made up of subatomic particles, which ebb and flow at varying rates of magnitude according to the harmonic resonance between them:

III. THE PRINCIPLE OF VIBRATION
Nothing rests; everything moves; everything vibrates.[4]

V. THE PRINCIPLE OF RHYTHM
Everything flows, out and in; everything has its tides; all things rise and fall; the pendulum-swing manifests in everything; the measure of the swing to the right is the measure of the swing to the left; rhythm compensates.[5]

Yet both of these are meaningless if they are not understood in relation to the first principle of Hermeticism, which indicates how there could be any fluctuations of vibration and rhythm in relation to spirit and matter. This principle states:

I. THE PRINCIPLE OF MENTALISM
THE ALL IS MIND; The Universe is Mental.[6]

Mind here should not be mistaken for the superficial mind, or ego, which is only an accumulation of conditioning. Rather this mind is consciousness, which is the foundation of the entire universe.

Modern spiritual and scientific understanding are coming to the same conclusion: that everything is a manifestation of a unified field of consciousness. Consciousness, according to the sages, is not isolated within the mind of the human brain, but exists everywhere in three planes, which are defined in the wisdom traditions as the physical, mental, and spiritual planes. The Hindu philosophy of Vedanta is in part based on the deep understanding that what we in the modern era know as the atom is actually a spiritual aspect of the one consciousness of Brahman (irreducible essence/ultimate reality/godhead), which functions like a breath coming from the spiritual plane into the manifestation of the physical plane. The spiritual atom is a product of consciousness and moves according to the focus of conscious awareness. My book *The Science and Practice of Humility* goes into this subject in depth.

Consciousness produces the spiritual atom, which multiplies through the principle of vibration and rhythm until we have the outward form of matter, which in essence is nothing more than a garment of consciousness manifested through the dance of subatomic particles. The physical, mental, and spiritual planes of consciousness are connected by the vibration and rhythm of subatomic particles producing the dance of life. Consciousness dwells in everything, both space and matter, in a cosmic symphony. The individual is part of this symphony, and synchronicity is the harmony that is produced by this dance. Yet only those who trust the universe can perceive this dance with clear eyes.

Synchronicity does exist for everyone, even materialists and nonbelievers. But the ignorant pass such experiences off as coincidence and do not learn or grow from them. One who dwells on the spiritual plane perceives things as they are in holistic truth, while one who is primarily on the mental and physical planes still believes in a material world devoid of spirit. In Confucius's commentary on the *I Ching,* he explains that what we resonate deeply with will affect our experience and, consequently, the synchronicity experienced between the underlying spirit of the individual and the external world:

> Things that accord in tone vibrate together. Things that have affinity in their inmost natures seek one another. Water flows to what is wet, fire turns to what is dry. Clouds (the breath of heaven) follow

the dragon, wind (the breath of earth) follows the tiger. Thus the sage arises, and all creatures follow him with their eyes. What is born of heaven feels related to what is above. What is born of earth feels related to what is below. Each follows its kind.[7]

Whatever our mind is focused on will be the world we experience, because perception is molded by life through the thoughts, feelings, and emotions that we hold as important to us. Although the spiritual plane influences both the mental and physical planes, thoughts, feelings, and emotions exist on the mental plane and cannot become pure unless one dwells on the spiritual plane. People who live only in the two lower worlds are driven by their conditioning; they are attracted only to those realms and suffer according to their apparent duality. On the other hand, those very few who live on the spiritual plane can see the one consciousness in harmony playing out in all forms. Chuang-tzu poetically explains this spiritual perception: "When there is no more separation between 'this' and 'that,' it is called the still-point of the Tao. At the still-point in the center of the circle one can see the infinite in all things."[8]

The spiritual understanding of consciousness also conflicts with the materialistic scientific perspective. Materialistic science is under the impression that consciousness is a phenomenon limited to the mind, which in turn is believed to be situated inside the brain. From this we can understand why synchronicity has not been given any serious thought in the scientific field outside of psychology and quantum physics.

To regard consciousness as merely the function of the physical anatomy of the brain resembles the religious notion that spirit and matter are separate. From a common-sense point of view, how could anything in life be connected or relate to anything else without consciousness? How could rain nourish plant life and plant life nourish us in turn if there were no underlying consciousness compelling them to do so? All manifestations of consciousness relate to each other in a symbiotic harmony, but usually only a sage can recognize it. Synchronicity brings this awareness to the forefront of our knowledge when our perception has been marinated in a trust in wu-wei and the harmony of Tao.

THE ORIGIN OF SYNCHRONICITY

Although all of this may explain how synchronicity can be experienced in one's life, it does not give us any indication of the origin of its existence. Questions about the origins of synchronicity arise when we compare the spiritual significance of the evolutionary process of the universe as opposed to the eternally present Self, which is not constricted by time, space, name, and form. People are often in a bind over these two apparently opposing realities. None of this confusion is new, as differing opinions have always arisen on this subject among the Hindus, Taoists, and Zen Buddhists.

In the Hindu philosophy of Vedanta they would argue that synchronicity is born of the Eternal Self/undifferentiated consciousness (Atman) and that it is only a phenomenon of change, which has no relation to the Eternal Self. The Zen master, for his part, would state that synchronicity appears as a phenomenon when we remain in the stillness of the Void (*sunyata* in Sanskrit) and could be thought of as a temporary illusion. The Taoists would assume that synchronicity is the result of some connection between the inner and outer worlds, but they could never give a definite reason about why it exists. Though all three insights may appear opposed, they are all in essence valid explanations and hint toward a single origin.

Patanjali's yoga of practice complemented by stillness gives us an indication of synchronicity's origins. Patanjali understood that the "doing" of practice is in alignment with the evolutionary unfolding, while the "nondoing" of stillness brings one in resonance with the

Eternal Self, which is the source of Tao within us. This is the Vedic wisdom that teaches Atman is Brahman. The aspects of doing and nondoing harmonize with each other and bring forth unity between the changing and the changeless, or in other words, between motion and stillness. This unified harmony, manifested on an individual level, is the origin of synchronicity.

Lao-tzu refers to a "Way" (Tao) that is found by few. The most common understanding of the Way is the course of things, which I've mentioned: if we follow it in life, it will guide us as if we were floating down a stream to the greater ocean. When a stream flows down a mountain, it finds its own path. Similarly, living in harmony with nature is finding your own way: this is the Way of the Tao. Even when we block the stream or resist it, it will find its own way, and we will suffer from swimming against the current.

Consider a fallen leaf that is flowing on a stream. If you, like the leaf, allow the stream to carry you in this fashion, its power becomes yours—te. You become one with nature, without clinging, without attachment, and leaving the past behind to live completely in the present moment. The Way in this context is a simple understanding of how one follows the evolutionary energies, or cosmic unfolding, of the universe. But it still does not indicate why it is imperative to follow the Way, nor does it address the reality of our Eternal Self, which is identical to the Tao/Brahman. Every tradition speaks of our eternal and real Self in different ways, but how does that relate to the common perspective of the Way?

The sages of practically all spiritual traditions would suggest that when we follow the Way, it eventually humbles us and softens our hearts, which gives us greater knowledge of the Eternal Self. Conversely, when one sincerely chooses to remain present as the Eternal Self in stillness or self-inquiry, as many Buddhist and Hindu teachers would suggest, one becomes aware of the Way.

So both apparently opposing spiritual perspectives reach the same destination, even though the journey is different. Whether you attempt to remain present in stillness as the Eternal Self or you follow the Way, you will reveal the other, as if they were the same thing. When we look into the Eternal Self we discover the Way, and when we follow the Way we reveal the Eternal Self. This sort of knowledge is only understood by those that Chuang-tzu would call the "spiritual elite." Only those who are sincere in their own introspection will understand how both the Eternal Self and the Way go together as one. If one does not know the experience of the Way or the Self, then all of this will appear as nothing more than words.

There is no difference between the cosmic unfolding and the Eternal Self, even though many people tend to think so. But they do not understand the wisdom of Lao-tzu because of their incorrect view of separateness between the Eternal Self and the Way. People tend to hold one form over the other while missing Lao-tzu's point of letting go. The origin and significance of synchronicity are revealed in the mirror of the Self and the Way.

The origin of synchronicity comes from the union of the Way and the Eternal Self. The Eternal Self and the Way go together as one, and this is experienced as synchronicity. Synchronicity is the language of Tao that manifests in an individual's life as a result of his or her harmony between the Eternal Self and the Way. In Vedanta, as I've mentioned, this is known as the connection between Atman (Eternal Self/ undifferentiated consciousness) and Brahman (irreducible essence/ ultimate reality). There is also the movement of energy in the manifest world (prakrti) and the stillness of pure awareness (Purusha) of the yogic philosophy of Patanjali.

One experiences synchronicity when both the Self and the Way are in perfect correspondence. Through the experience of synchronicity one understands that one is in accord with the Tao both within oneself and in the evolutionary unfolding of the universe. This is the "real" Way of the Tao that Lao-tzu and other ancient masters referred to.

The Way of the Tao, then, is the Way of the Self. If you are sincere in exploring yourself, then the peaceful resonance of synchronicity will begin to bring magic to your life. The Way of the Self, or Tao, is to completely follow the reality of wu-wei into a future that is unknown. Synchronicity is our safe guide into the wilderness of the universe. In this wilderness we discover that the Eternal Self and the Way are like everything else—unified. The essential wisdom of Lao-tzu is that everything goes together, but this truth only dawns on those who follow wu-wei. Sages do not bring Heaven to Earth by building upon what has already been established. On the contrary, they deconstruct what has been built by remaining small through simplicity and the power of uselessness.

10

Nothing Is More Useless
than Wu-Wei

A life of humility, simplicity, and spontaneity is generally thought of as a useless and purposeless approach to living. Yet something as sublime as synchronicity cannot be experienced unless one is faithful to what is taken to be useless. Synchronicity spontaneously emerges out of a void of nothingness, which brings the magic of the universe to life. What we assume to be useless contains the greatest potential within its incomprehensibility. The unconscious is never considered to be a reality of our existence, so it is cast off as a useless preoccupation of the spiritually confused. But that "useless" unconscious conspires with fate in bringing to life the miracle of synchronicity and a relationship with Tao. In investing time and energy only into the physical parts of life, excessively striving to achieve our so-called goals, we discard the ineffable space that holds the universe in its place.

The common human perspective, conditioned and time-bound in the world of form, regards space as nothing to take into consideration. But we see that this perspective is a narrow one when we realize that the universe is predominantly space compared to the infinitely smaller world of matter. We consider space as useless because there is nothing we can do with it. The human mind desires to shape the world according to its personal cravings and beliefs, so it would never conceive the eternal importance of useless space. We can easily contemplate the world of form and continue to explore its depths. But when we take into consideration space and its eternal presence, the mind is brought to a screeching halt. In this confusion, we tend to condemn the unknowable with the label of uselessness.

What we can mold with our hands and influence with our minds is, to many people, the only issue of general importance. Yet we are overlooking the absurdly obvious fact that life emerges out of space, not the other way around. The outer fringes of the universe, which is the physical world, is what is of least importance to a sage. The essential wisdom of Lao-tzu would suggest that the insignificant in life is the significant. We assume that we have no use for space, but physical and mental existence could not be alive without it. From our narrow perspective, we generally exclude the other side of anything, but a consciousness or spirituality that is not inclusive and integral is destined for failure. Lao-tzu knew this spiritual failure all too well, and this is why he urged individuals simply to follow the Way of the Tao. This nondoing and this unattached mode of consciousness would bring the totality of the universe back into harmony through the wisdom of what is useless.

Space in all of its reality is rarely given any serious thought. Yet when we peek into the useless, we gain a better understanding of the total picture. We cannot understand life by living only in the world of objects. To discard the useless in favor of the useful is a grave mistake. The uselessness of space in our everyday lives is ever-present almost in the same fashion as the unconscious. All aspects of life that we either enjoy or attempt to ignore exist in the vastness of space. Reading these very words can only be possible because space is a reality connecting the world of form. Space in this context is everywhere we look. Whether it be between people or stars, space is there in its so-called useless capacity.

USELESS SPACE IS USEFUL

In Lao-tzu's Taoism, space is still thought of as useless. But the difference is that uselessness is embraced, because it holds the secret of the universe within its unknowability.

From this perspective, Lao-tzu's value system is the polar opposite of what the majority of humanity finds valuable. For example, when we look at something as simple as a cup, what is valuable about it? In many cases, people would believe the cup itself is valuable, but this is merely an illusion. The cup itself has no value, because it is the space within the cup that gives it value. We never consider that if it were not for the space within the cup, we could not enjoy a beverage of any variety. When we perceive space in this way, we find its undiscovered value everywhere in our lives and in the most simple places. We adore our homes, for example, for the craftsmanship and architecture that make us feel comfortable and secure. Yet it is not the walls of the house that give it value; again, it is the space within the walls that allows us to have comfort. The value comes from the space that is incorrectly deemed as useless.

To understand the metaphorical value of space and uselessness, it is best to turn to the greatest exponent of this wisdom, Chuang-tzu. In the truest essence of Tao, Chuang-tzu would always bring our attention to what we generally ignore. He consistently and skillfully points out the absolute necessity of what is of apparently no use. For Chuang-tzu, what is useless is somehow a parable for knowing the Tao. In Thomas Merton's brilliant book *The Way of Chuang Tzu*, we read:

> *Hui Tzu said to Chuang Tzu:*
> *"All your teaching is centered on what has no use."*

Chuang Tzu replied:
"If you have no appreciation for what has no use
You cannot begin to talk about what can be used.
The earth, for example, is broad and vast
But of all this expanse a man uses only a few inches
Upon which he happens to be standing.
Now suppose you suddenly take away
All that he is not actually using
So that, all round his feet a gulf
Yawns, and he stands in the Void,
With nowhere solid except right under each foot:
How long will he be able to use what he is using?"

Hui Tzu said: "It would cease to serve any purpose."

Chuang Tzu concluded:
"This shows
The absolute necessity
Of what has 'no use.'"[1]

Chuang-tzu brings clarity to our distorted view of what should be obvious. Although we usually take into account only that which is "useful," through clarity we realize that everything has value. In this way, Chuang-tzu is subtly saying that what we do not know or conceive of is actually what has value and what is of most importance. Chuang-tzu valued the so-called ugliness of life. This is why he commended the hunchback, the useless tree, and everything that we assume is vile and uncomfortable in the world. His "useless tree" analogy, found in the *Chuang-tzu* text, encapsulates the depth of wisdom that the useless conceals:

Tzu-ch'i of Nan-po was wandering around the Hill of Shang when he saw a huge tree there, different from all the rest. A thousand teams of horses could have taken shelter under it and its shade would have covered them all. Tzu-ch'i said, "What tree is this? It must certainly have some extraordinary usefulness!" But, looking up, he saw that the smaller limbs were gnarled and twisted, unfit for beams or rafters, and looking down, he saw that the trunk was pitted and rotten and could not be used for coffins. He licked one of the leaves and it blistered his mouth and made it sore. He sniffed the odor and it was enough to make a man drunk for three days. "It turns out to be a completely unusable tree," said Tzu-ch'i, "and so it has been able to grow this big. Aha!—it is this unusableness that the Holy Man makes use of!"[2]

At first Tzu-ch'i perceived something that was of no use, but then he could step back and see the beauty of what is within the superficially ugly. That useless tree grew big in its flexibility and nourished "all" in doing so. This is the "aha" moment of realization for Tzu-ch'i, because the useless tree is a metaphor for the wisdom that is concealed within a holy individual or sage. The useless space in the holy sage is the emptiness within the psychological faculties and the spiritual nature of consciousness. The nothingness of space corresponds to the nature of our mind, which is emptiness, or nothingness. To a world built on intellectual pursuits and egotistical cravings, an empty mind is a useless mind. Yet because the essence and nature of consciousness is space, when we become as empty as space we have the capacity to contain the entire universe as space does. Pure consciousness, Purusha, is the reflection of eternal space. The useless-tree analogy functions in correspondence to this eternal pure consciousness.

Comparing the useless tree to a sage, we understand that this tree, being useless, can grow to an immensity in size, flexible, with no particular structure, and is able to nourish and give shelter to all who come under it. The sage, by comparison, acknowledges and reveres the useless things in life, both within and without, while living a simple and humble life that many people would regard as small and insignificant. Yet this small and content life allows the light of Tao to grow and shine brightly in a world of ignorance. In this state, a sage is as receptive as space, because he has no dogma or belief system to restrict his awareness from allowing all experience to happen without resistance. This receptive, feminine, yin trust in the universe nourishes humanity, because people begin to take shelter under the sage's wisdom. In emptying the faculties of conditioning, a sage becomes a beacon of light for the Tao to move through to inspire others with its wisdom, bringing the world back into harmony.

SIMPLE LIVING AND THE
POWER OF HUMILITY

To know the Tao is to explore the useless space within ourselves and begin the "yoking" process of what we mistakenly assume is our identity. Our conditioned personality obscures the Way of the Tao, because we believe that if we act within the limitations of our beliefs, we will be useful. Although you may be useful for maintaining the hypnosis of the world, you will be of no use for the Tao to shine through. When we begin to yoke the will of our conditioned personality, te, the virtuous power of the divine will, begins to reinstate its proper place within us. An honest attitude of receptivity and simple living brings forth a transcendent humility. Although this is small in stature, it transforms the world. This is Lao-tzu's wisdom of seeking the low places:

> *The supreme good is like water,*
> *which nourishes all things without trying to.*
> *It is content with the low places that people disdain.*
> *Thus it is like the Tao.*

In dwelling, live close to the ground.
In thinking, keep to the simple.
In conflict, be fair and generous.
In governing, don't try to control.
In work, do what you enjoy.
In family life, be completely present.

When you are content to be simply yourself
and don't compare or compete,
everybody will respect you.[3]

This humility results from the power of te, the virtue of the divine will, which softens one's rigid personality and enables one to accept the world and everybody else for what and who they are.

Accepting the world and other people is unattainable from within our conditioned personalities. We judge everything according to our beliefs, and as a result we cannot clearly perceive the still point of the Tao. But in the power of sincere humility, a sage meets everybody on common ground and can address any problem, whether physical, mental, or spiritual. A sage can only be a sage if she has this capacity for receptivity and does not shy away from the spiritually ignorant. Residing in the infinite depth of the void of nothingness, a sage is like the useless tree, under whose wisdom people take shelter and are guided on the path to liberation. This becomes a mirror reflection of the Tao. The Tao loves and nourishes all, and so does the sage, because her personality, polluted with petty beliefs, cravings, and desires, has evaporated into thin air, and she naturally exhibits loving traits such as compassion, empathy, and forgiveness.

Sages, appearing useless, are often left alone by the populace to live their lives as they choose. Embracing uselessness gets us closer to liberation and enlightenment. In Taoist wisdom, this is thought of as a formula for longevity, which is true in some sense. Those who are focused on long life can learn a lot from the useless tree of Chuang-tzu. For example, the useless tree was bigger than any other tree, its branches and trunk were all crooked and contorted, its leaves were not nutritious, so this tree was left alone to live out its life, as it was of no use to the crafty and scheming people of the world. A straight and rigid tree, on the other hand, lives a very different life from the useless tree. The straight and rigid tree is thought of as useful because we can use its wood for building houses, boats, tables, and so on. Such a tree is usually cut down in its prime. Furthermore, trees who are trying to stand above the rest are often cut down first. The straight and rigid, useful tree is a metaphor for righteous people, who attempt to change the world according to their belief systems.

We are not here to condemn the righteous, but what we discover in this comparison is that those who are righteous are usually forcing their will over the world, and in some cases they tragically lose their life too early as a result. The wise, who correspond to the useless tree, grow old through not forcing themselves upon anything. Their simple humility secretly transforms the world without any intention to do so.

Now let us consider the useless and useful trees in regard to the psychological and spiritual planes of consciousness. In these contexts, we can see that this straightness and rigidness equates to the concrete conditioning that we formulate about ourselves throughout life. The tendency toward righteousness and harboring personal agendas is the result of a rigid mind. This rigid mind in turn causes pain, suffering, and conflict at all levels. A world built on such narrowness of mind can use such individuals, but their consciousness will be drained and kept from a connection with Tao. Our admiration for people clothed in the rigid attire of a suit and necktie replicates this narrowness of mind. These mental limitations ensure that we will be accepted by others in a godless world, where materialism and monetary success are king.

The wise sage, on the other hand, grows as big as the useless tree, both psychologically and spiritually, because the immensity of the Tao is moving through his empty, unattached, and effortless mind. What the average individual would assume is useless is precisely what the Tao makes use of. Indeed the Tao can only make use of the useless; as with the empty cup, space is the true value that the Tao uses, and toward which it gravitates. The *Chuang-tzu* text explains, "The Way gathers in emptiness alone. Emptiness is the fasting of the mind."[4]

The Tao cannot make use of a useful mind that is filled to the brim, because there is no room for the Tao to shine through. Recognizing how the Tao moves in life, Lao-tzu and Chuang-tzu admired uselessness. They experienced the stream of the Tao, which moves toward that which has no obstruction.

When the mental plane begins to marinate in the spiritual plane, a lucid openness becomes our prevalent attitude toward life. The trust we have longed for dawns on us when we have become humble in our receptivity to the universe. In general this open state of consciousness is thought of as weak. Yet this nonforcing way of life brings us to the most useless aspect of life.

Nothing is more useless than wu-wei. When we do not force life, we are not being useful in the busy world of doing. A mind full of effort is applauded over an effortless mind. Nondoing is a laughable way of living, according to people in general. It is the most useless way of being that anyone can conceive of. Yet the act of leaving things alone allows the Tao to bring harmony into the world without our personal interference.

The useless teaching of Chuang-tzu is precisely to live wu-wei, it is the only sane solution for all the individual and collective issues in our world. And yet wu-wei should not be thought of as a cure to an illness, because our natural state of consciousness *is* wu-wei; the problem is simply that we have ceased to live it in the modern day. In not living it, we can never truly love, as our deep-seated hatred, the result of our conditioning, activates the deluded mind into a propensity toward doing alone.

The illusion of separation comes from the active side of life, because we do not trust the Way of the Tao. The greatest expression of love is beyond the personal; it is unconditionally and universally beyond concept and form. To leave things alone and let life run its own course is how unconditional love comes into the world. The unity of humankind can be achieved no other way, because any other way is an act of division, being based on force.

As I have mentioned, the unity of oneness, which enlightens our consciousness into nirvana, can only become our reality when we trust. This trust is unconditional love, and a new world can be born when this harmonic resonance between trust and love begins to bear fruit within humanity. To live in any other state than trust is absurd when we realize that the world that you and I live in is the same. When we overcome our hypnotic conditioning, we understand that in unity there can be a sincere love for all in the same sense that Jesus urged us to love thy neighbor. Yet we have to live this love, and this can only be done through trust. We cannot truly love each other without wu-wei.

11

Living Wu-Wei in the Tao of a New World

One might assume that Lao-tzu's essential wisdom of wu-wei is too lofty and impractical to have any relationship to love or to the unity of humanity. From our usual understanding of life, we cannot fathom how nondoing can benefit us, individually or collectively. We believe that everything we have in this world is the outcome of force and striving. As a result, our perspective on life and love has not transcended our personal agendas. According to Lao-tzu, this is fundamentally obvious, so he searched for an understanding of life that would transmute love from the limitations of the personal into the limitless love of the universal.

Living wu-wei does not mean retreating to a cave or a forest to live life in isolation—something Chuang-tzu understood completely, as he remained in society. Though at the beginning of living wu-wei there is usually a propensity to seek isolation—and in some sense this is necessary—invariably one will yearn to return to the world to continue to live wu-wei, which is a great act of compassion. The essential wisdom of Lao-tzu has no definite form or application. It varies according to the temperament of the individual. One who fully comprehends wu-wei understands that developing healthy relationships with other people is the spiritual adhesive that harmonizes the Tao among humanity.

We cannot learn more about ourselves without others, as they reveal psychological tendencies that we have not dealt with. But this does not mean that we should go seeking to find relationships, as would be the case with a doctrine such as Confucianism. Nor does this mean we should seek an excessive amount of friends. Any relationship we have in life should develop organically and grow of itself. There is no right or wrong method here. One only needs to reveal to oneself the significance of living wu-wei.

FLOWING AGAINST THE TAO OF LOVE

The metaphysical and spiritual depth of the *Tao Te Ching* is not aimed at nondoing for the sake of being lazy and playing no part in the drama of life. On the contrary, living wu-wei truly reveals a unity and universal love for all. But this should not be confused with the universal love of Confucianism, which we are supposed to attempt to induce, as if the Way of the Tao could be coerced by our personal will. The Tao loves and nourishes all without the need for our persuasion. Yet the Way only becomes a subtle reality in the life of one who has begun to purge his consciousness of the psychological attractions and distractions of the external world, which disconnect our mind from the Tao.

In fact, our entire culture is built on distracting the mind away from this connection with the higher intelligence of the universe. Day to day, we primarily focus our attention on the temporal reality rather than the essence of life. Disassociated from eternity, we use nature unthinkingly, like a public toilet, and we treat people in the same way, which causes disharmonic repercussions around the world. We attempt to heal these repercussions from the same temporal outlook, which only causes more damage, rather than letting the situation sort itself out organically so that it can eventually subside.

Real love is a prisoner in this world of temporary delights and can only be freed in the realization of wu-wei. We perceive love only in relation to wife, husband, child, mother, father, brother, sister, and friends. Yet this is a limited understanding of love, as it is only the result of association with people we are familiar and intimate with. This does not mean that the love you have for your family and friends is not love; it *is* love. But the problem arises when we cannot extend the love we feel for our family and friends beyond those parameters. None of this is inherently the individual's fault, because we have built a divisive society, which is incorrectly assumed to be a community.

This division from one another is the creation of the mindless crowd, who wander around, isolated from everybody else. We are not only divided by religions and nations, but we are also separate from other individuals. Religious, nationalistic, and cultural beliefs keep individuals isolated, as they fear other people who may conflict with their narrow perceptions of the world. Hence many people in our world drop to their knees and bow to the artificial world instead of to the natural world. This is a psychosis developed from identification with artificial constraints.

We become slaves to the unnatural world because we mistake its artificiality with nature and assume that nation, religion, race, or gender, which are components of the unnatural world, are actually somehow intrinsic to our real self. The Way of the Tao will only be known when we have let go of what corrupts our nature. The value system of our world is corrupt because we believe that a world that is divided is natural and harmonious. Nothing could be further from the truth, especially when we realize that all of the tyranny and bloodshed on this planet is the result of such separation. Indeed the common valuations of success are detrimental to the survival of the human race, because they are based on servitude to a life that is diametrically opposed to nature and to an individual's li.

Success as understood in our current system of values suppresses human nature. We succumb to servitude so we can acquire the material possessions that are supposed to validate success. Yet, as we know, this form of success is ephemeral and fake. We also seek salvation through artificial means, especially technological devices such as televisions, computers, and phones. What we seek through these devices, though, reveals our internal struggle, because our suppressed nature holds a repressed anger, which we stimulate through vicarious violence.

Violence becomes socially accepted when we go against our nature and block the integral universal flow of Tao. The violence we seek through entertainment and the news discloses the frustration we harbor within as a result of our empty, uncreative lives. We are attracted to acts of violence because they reflect our inner turmoil. The senseless brutality and cruelty of wars, genocide, and random acts of violence have all become nothing more than daily entertainment for one to parrot one's opinion about in mindless exchanges with others who are also parroting opinion.

Desensitization has led our species into a psychotic numbness that feels nothing for the bloodshed of our brothers and sisters around the world. How could our love ever become free from the personal if we still dwell within our brutal animal mind? In such a world, violence becomes normal behavior, which we express both physically and mentally. As a result of this attraction to violence, many people cringe at the sight of physical acts of love. The suppression of our li nature has desensitized our whole being not only to acts of hatred but also to those of love.

We need to ask, then, what is more dangerous in our world, hatred or love? We would never want to admit to ourselves that it is far easier to hate life than it is to love life. But this is the behavior of those who are distracted from their union with Tao and its Way. In such a world, physical and mental expressions of love are far more dangerous than expressions of physical and mental hatred. A society that works on this assumption is insane. It is devoted not to the survival of the human race but to the destruction of life. Alan Watts comments:

> Inability to accept the mystic experience is more than an intellectual handicap. Lack of awareness of the basic unity of organism and environment is a serious and dangerous hallucination. For in a civilization equipped with immense technological power, the sense of alienation between man and nature leads to the use of technology in a hostile spirit—to the "conquest" of nature instead of intelligent cooperation with nature.[1]

Working against the nature of Tao, both within and without, leaves humanity in a place of desperate survival. We believe we are disconnected from one another. Disharmony on all fronts is the outcome, and as a result many people find themselves only cognizant of time-bound emotional love. Isolating love in this way leads humanity into numerous forms of segregation. The harmony of Tao cannot be a reality within our being and in the world if our love does not move out of the emotional and into the universal. How could we love our neighbors if we are concerned only for those we regard as useful, without any consideration for those we think of as useless? How can we possibly reconnect with the Way of the Tao if we are nothing more than part of a mindless crowd in no real communion with one another?

ENLIGHTENING THE SHADOW THROUGH HARMONIC RELATIONSHIPS

Contrary to popular belief, Lao-tzu's Taoism is not about escaping from society to abide in isolation away from people. Chuang-tzu exemplifies this best, as he remained in society and did not refrain from auspicious meetings with others. The Tao of Lao-tzu is primarily about the trust of wu-wei, which includes a trust in our relationship and connection with humanity. Feeling and knowing the Tao more through wu-wei means that one is building harmony on all levels, especially within humanity.

Developing a relationship with people outside of our emotional center is the best way to understand our vasanas, the psychological habits and tendencies that drive our karma and block us from the encompassing transparency of enlightenment. Authentic Taoists know this best, because they have given their lives over to wu-wei and welcome all that unfolds as their experience, especially with relationships. Even though Buddhist and Hindu monks advocate a monastic life as a way of attaining liberation, many Buddhist and Hindu masters will admit that there are some aspects of our being that we cannot work through without being engaged in intimate relationships. While a monastic life has its benefits and will transform your consciousness, it is more medicinal than dietary. To close yourself off permanently from humanity can be viewed as the grossest act of negation and ignorance that one could exhibit, because one is only content in finding God within and so ignores the reality of discovering God in the world.

If we are to expand our consciousness, it is imperative that we experience the fullness of life in a way by which we can learn and grow from these experiences. The escapes of animalistic sex, alcohol, drugs, chronic negativity, and so on, are not in themselves bad, because these addictions reveal deeper aspects about ourselves that they attempt to suppress. Addictions tend to teach us a lot about ourselves. Of course I am not advocating for addictions, but purification is not possible without learning from our cultural tendency to become addicted. Addiction is another paradox of life, and it is something all of us have experienced sometime. Addictions vary only in degree, from alcohol to television, and according to what is socially accepted. Of course the media and other unnatural systems, such as government, do not view television as an addiction, because it keeps people blindly following their agendas.

Addiction at this time—and we can think of all negative emotions as addictions—is still a part of the world, whether we like it or not, and only a sincere individual will weed out any addiction, no matter how subtle. The big problem in monastic life is that any addiction is perceived as faulty and something to be overcome through repetitive practice. For example, certain Buddhist teachers perceive anger as a bad emotion that students should push to the side and not identify with. Yet anger in itself is a healthy, reactive emotion that we acquired through evolution to help us survive, and it will always come into the field of consciousness when circumstances permit.

Buddhism uses mindfulness to cleanse an individual of the habit of falling into aggression. But we also need to keep in mind that when anger is pushed away with no mindfulness, aggression can result. An individual can be angry in a compassionate context, as happens almost every day when one empathizes and sympathizes with another's situation. However our suppression of anger in the world makes us incapable of love, as the seeds of our anger continue to grow roots deep within us that, unless acknowledged, often turn into unconscious aggression. To be mindful of our anger and to be able to express it to another without being aggressive will transform anger into love.

Psychologically, repressing our anger, or any emotion, without making it mindful has a devastating effect both on the individual and on the collective. Many people who are spiritually inclined tend to suppress dark aspects within themselves, incorrectly assuming that these emotions are illusory, fearful, and negative. Instead of moving through their pain, they store it in the back closet of their minds, where it continues to grow stronger.

This suppression is called "spiritual bypassing," a term first coined by the American psychotherapist John Welwood back in 1984.

Canadian spiritual psychotherapist Robert Augustus Masters explains this problem in his book *Spiritual Bypassing:*

> Spiritual bypassing is the use of spiritual practices and beliefs to avoid dealing with our painful feelings, unresolved wounds, and developmental needs. It is much more common than we might think and, in fact, is so pervasive as to go largely unnoticed, except in its more obvious extremes.
>
> Part of the reason for this is that we tend not to have very much tolerance, either personally or collectively, for facing, entering, and working through our pain, strongly preferring pain-numbing "solutions," regardless of how much suffering such "remedies" may catalyze. Because this preference has so deeply and thoroughly infiltrated our culture that it has become all but normalized, spiritual bypassing fits almost seamlessly into our collective habit of turning away from what is painful, as a kind of higher analgesic with seemingly minimal side effects. It is a spiritualized strategy not only for avoiding pain but also for legitimizing such avoidance, in ways ranging from the blatantly obvious to the extremely subtle.
>
> Spiritual bypassing is a very persistent shadow of spirituality, manifesting in many forms, often without being acknowledged as such. Aspects of spiritual bypassing include exaggerated detachment, emotional numbing and repression, overemphasis on the positive, anger-phobia, blind or overly tolerant compassion, weak or too porous boundaries, lopsided development (cognitive intelligence often being far ahead of emotional and moral intelligence), debilitating judgment about one's negativity or shadow side, devaluation of the personal relative to the spiritual, and delusions of having arrived at a higher level of being.[2]

The traits of spiritual bypassing are strongest in those who have practiced spiritual cultivation and followed a spiritual philosophy in an attempt to eliminate karma and the vasanas on the mental and physical planes of consciousness. We discover this in many ashrams, temples, monasteries, synagogues, and churches around the world, where both the student and the master will be very rigid in their beliefs and will be unreceptive to a new perspective. This is why many people who stay in sacred places for some time become aware of the deep-seated bad temper of the master, especially when his authority has been threatened. But one who is truly a master will always listen with an open mind and heart, in a place of neutrality toward all people. Of course, it is sometimes a great act of compassion when a master scolds a layman or disciple for being unconscious in their words, thoughts, and deeds, or even when they misunderstand a philosophical concept or teaching. Only a master in a place of neutrality will know when such actions are beneficial.

Practicing spiritual cultivation in the hope that our psychological pain will somehow disappear is absurd. As we learn from the Eastern perspective, we need to own and understand our pain so we can eventually grow out of it, which is the true meaning of transcendence. Enlightenment depends on a total comprehension of our being, including the functioning of the physical body and the operation of the mind. Spiritual bypassing becomes a reality when we do not deal with that aspect of our consciousness that Carl Jung called the *shadow*, which is that part of ourselves that we deny and avoid seeing. When we are engaged in deep spiritual practice without backing it up with complementary shadow work, we have little chance of growing into an authentic enlightenment.

Those who have only a partially spiritual approach to life often show increasing habits of spiritual pride. This spiritual pride is identical with the pride of many athletes. We often get caught in our own spiritual concepts and build a totally new persona around the means of liberation rather than the end (eating the menu once again). The social harmony Confucius pined for cannot come to fruition if we are not prepared to work through our personal shadow elements. And shadow work cannot be undertaken successfully without connection with other people. Relationships of any variety are the best for bringing the shadow to the light of consciousness. Although many people will avoid uncomfortable relationships, in many cases these are the very things that will be able to mirror shadow elements that we have not made conscious.

But keep in mind that this does not mean *everything* is about you. Sometimes people are a certain way because they themselves have unresolved psychological problems that are in no way related to you. For example, someone can be violent, cynical, or self-centered. These things may have nothing to do with you, but instead are the flaws in the other individual. Avoiding one's own pain is revealed in relationships on a very deep and subtle level of the psyche. It does not usually take the gross form of people with bad attitudes, so please don't make everything about yourself.

Spiritually inclined people are not exempt from this avoidance. Often they are more susceptible to this than the average individual. Those who live monastic lives often exhibit a lack of shadow work, as they continue to avoid relationships with which they don't personally resonate. But any deep spiritual work should bring into our consciousness a unity and feeling of oneness within that correlates to the world without. We cannot eliminate one from the other if we truly yearn for liberation. If you are intentionally avoiding relationships, you are still bound to fear, no matter who you believe you are. (Keep in mind that I am not advocating that you uphold a relationship with a toxic person who has a track record of bringing you down.)

Accepting yourself and others as they are is one of the greatest expressions of love one can show, and it actually has the power to energetically harmonize any relationship, no matter how broken it may be. Accepting our pain and owning it brings spiritual light into our shadow so we can become that jewel within the lotus flower. But none of this can happen if we continue to spiritually bypass our pain and avoid relationships in fearful isolation. The spiritually mature understand that isolation is only useful when seekers can bring what they have learned about themselves back into humanity.

Much of what our modern spirituality has become is a very self-centered approach to liberation. For example, Advaita Vedanta is probably the most popular and dominant school of Hindu philosophy and practice. The essence of Advaita Vedanta is a practice of abiding as the transcendental Self, Atman, which is undifferentiated pure consciousness, so one can eventually realize the ultimate reality, Brahman, which is also pure consciousness. This is attained, or rediscovered, through sincere self-inquiry into one's nature. Advaita Vedanta, then, is a philosophy of nondualism, the nonduality of Atman and Brahman.

Advaita Vedanta gained public attention through Sri Ramana Maharshi, as he was one individual of modern times who really experienced liberation. Astonishingly, many followers of this beautiful path parrot Ramana Maharshi or other teachers, and in a lot of cases outwardly mimic the life of Ramana, without realizing that he was unique and so are they. Such parroting and mimicking results in a self-centered inquiry.

To realize the Self, as Ramana did, does not mean to eliminate the world from your reality. To inquire into the nature of your existence does not mean becoming a rigid guardian defending yourself against thoughts, feelings, and emotions. This incorrect approach to self-inquiry has led many individuals around the world to enter a blank, empty state. This is not the spirit of receptivity and humility. Instead it is a state of forcing oneself to be a certain way, in this case, forcing oneself to be empty for the sake of that desire, as if somehow a blank state of consciousness leads one to liberation.

The depths of Advaita Vedanta do not lie only in self-inquiry, a fact that many people misunderstand. The Sanskrit words *vasanas* and *samskaras,* which I have mentioned, both relate to how we deal with the mind and shadow work. *Vasanas* again refers to habitual ways and latent tendencies that one needs to own and work through in order to reach a higher state of consciousness. This in turn will transform our samskaras, our subliminal psychological imprints and mental impressions. Facing our vasanas and samskaras—another term for shadow work—is in no way separate from self-inquiry. If self-inquiry, or any other path, merely meant to attain a blank emotionless state without any capacity to relate to the world, then realizing the Self and liberation would appear pointless. But authentic liberation is not like this, because it comprehends the total sphere of consciousness, including the physical, mental, and spiritual planes of consciousness. Realizing the Eternal Self, Atman, within is not complete until you realize the Eternal Self also in the world. When the Way of the Tao is perceived, then the union of both Self within and the Self underlying the world of things begins to take place.

EMBRACING THE WORLD

The heart of Eastern wisdom teaches you to be naturally in the world without rejecting it. Many spiritual paths condemn and judge the world, as if they were enabling one to move beyond desires. But many fail to realize that they are desiring not to desire (a point that the Buddha understood). Lao-tzu saw all these pursuits of desiring not to desire as nothing more than spiritual pride and a moving away from our human nature. The Taoist perspective is to leave no stone unturned in an embrace of life and yourself, as exemplified by Chuang-tzu. He dived headfirst into life, bringing his internal harmony into the world and time in which he lived. In the introduction to *The Complete Works of Chuang Tzu* Burton Watson states:

> In Chuang Tzu's view, the man who has freed himself from conventional standards of judgment can no longer be made to suffer, for he

refuses to recognize poverty as any less desirable then affluence, to recognize death as any less desirable than life. He does not in any literal sense withdraw and hide from the world—to do so would show that he still passed judgment upon the world. He remains within society but refrains from acting out of the motives that lead ordinary men to struggle for wealth, fame, success, or safety. He maintains a state that Chuang Tzu refers to as *wu-wei,* or inaction, meaning by this term not a forced quietude, but a course of action that is not founded upon any purposeful motives of gain or striving. In such a state, all human actions become as spontaneous and mindless as those of the natural world. Man becomes one with Nature, or Heaven, as Chuang Tzu calls it, and merges himself with Tao, or the Way, the underlying unity that embraces man, Nature, and all that is in the universe.

To describe this mindless, purposeless mode of life, Chuang Tzu turns most often to the analogy of the artist or craftsman. The skilled woodcarver, the skilled butcher, the skilled swimmer does not ponder or ratiocinate on the course of action he should take; his skill has become so much a part of him that he merely acts instinctively and spontaneously and, without knowing why, achieves success. Again, Chuang Tzu employs the metaphor of a totally free and purposeless journey, using the word *yu* ("to wander" or "a wandering") to designate the way in which the enlightened man wanders through all of creation, enjoying its delights without ever becoming attached to any one part of it.[3]

Chuang-tzu never once condemned the world. Instead he used his insightfully witty humor to shine a light on wu-wei, which the world has unceremoniously put away in the closet. The Way of Lao-tzu has nothing to do with transcending desires, as this would be spiritual pride. But he is also not saying one should become lazy or sloppy and succumb to desires. What Lao-tzu is saying is that when we inquire not only into our own nature but also into the nature of the world, we will come into contact with the nature of the human heart, which is the nature of the universe, and that is love.

This love that is hidden within the heart of Lao-tzu's Taoism is not a love that one discovers and keeps for oneself. It is a love that is shared because, in the Taoist philosophy of li, this love, which transcends any boundary, will bring harmony to the world piece by piece, or perhaps I should say "peace by peace." The Way of Tao that an individual experiences brings this love into the world, and it inspires others, no matter how rigid their beliefs. This love, which all spiritual paths contend is the fruit of an enlightened soul, is not attainable if we do not accept ourselves and the world and gain a total comprehension of our inner and outer worlds.

The complete scope of Lao-tzu's Taoism is hard to fathom, as each individual is unique. But we do know that it is one of the only spiritual paths that has no set doctrine, dogma, or formulas, and this gives it the lucidity to reach every aspect of our consciousness. Lao-tzu's Taoism acknowledges the shadow, especially in the sense that one discovers one's intrinsic relationship to others and the world with no preconceived idea of how they should be, which allows for a great deal of transformation to occur and take us through our repressed pain.

One of the primary purposes of the *I Ching* is to understand the total picture of our psychology, which is why Jung was so attracted by it. When we have worked sincerely within ourselves and made conscious and accepted everything about ourselves, then we have truly become human and are able to sympathize with the pain of others through our humble hearts. Anything other than a true humble heart, in the eyes of Lao-tzu, would be catastrophic to the world. No relationship to another or to the world can be developed if we still own a personal agenda and have not embraced our pain.

Living wu-wei is the medicine for our ills in this world. Trusting and accepting ourselves and others is the remedy for building healthy, harmonious relationships, not only with one another, but also with the natural environment. An agendaless individual, working through the spiritual barriers within her own being, brings the wisdom of Tao into the world. In knowing ourselves, we can relate to other people and feel our integral connection not only to nature but also to the entire universe.

Any relationship we have with an individual, nature, or the cosmos can only be genuine and harmonious if we trust their intrinsic nature. Those who live wu-wei understand this best, because allowing life to be as it will brings equilibrium to the world, as one reflects the untouched purity, stillness, and aliveness of nature. Only when you understand that your real nature is wu-wei will you be able to have a relationship not only with yourself but with the entire universe in all of its glory.

WU-WEI'S NATURAL FLOW OF TAO

Our greatest relationship becomes a reality when we live wu-wei. This greatest of the great relationships is with the Tao, the Way of nature, which is our nature, Atman, which is Brahman. When we live wu-wei, we become aware of, and experience, ourselves in relation to the Way. No form of scientific study or speculation can ever calculate this reality, yet we know it is real, because we live it and feel it. Living it is being in harmony with that greatest of all relationships. This Way of nature is experienced by living wu-wei, as wu-wei is the essence of the universe.

In the world that we live in now, with ecological destruction for the sake of material possessions and with the divisions among humanity, a return to our wu-wei nature is imperative, or we will face the dire consequences of our ignorant actions. The way we commonly act toward each other and the planet is staggering evidence that we at this moment in time function as nothing more than machines that are hell-bent on destroying anything that conflicts with our greed and yearning for power. This state of deep sleep keeps us in our own private worlds, because we believe that we are constantly in a mode of survival against everything else. This belief unknowingly binds us to the animal kingdom, but if we can let go of this fear, we can finally become human.

The systems we have built perpetuate this isolation. Many religions, for example, eliminate God from the world because a God that is known to be universal, both within and without, conflicts with a lot of religious doctrines, which are built on a kind of political view of the universe, in which God is a king or lord, making people easy to control. This is truly a hypnotic view of reality, because everything in this world, including human beings, is part of nature, so how could God be excluded from anything? We have not even mentioned our relationship to planetary and universal forces that affect our minds, which is the essence of astrology. How could cosmic forces play a part in the consciousness of this planet unless these forces are part of God? The limitations of religion, science, and philosophy are destroying our minds, because anything built with boundaries, although it may work within those boundaries, in actual fact has nothing to do with the essence of an eternal God.

Bringing back into the awareness that God is both within us and in nature was at the heart of Lao-tzu's Taoism. Working with nature instead of going against it aligns us with the Tao, which allows this higher state of consciousness to produce conditions whereby others will also realize the Tao through their own nature. The English mystical philosopher and writer Aldous Huxley expresses this in his book *The Perennial Philosophy,* where he beautifully explains our ignorance of God *in* the world through a story from the *Chuang-tzu* text:

> The doctrine that God is in the world has an important practical corollary—the sacredness of Nature, and the sinfulness and folly of

man's overweening efforts to be her master rather than her intelligently docile collaborator. Sub-human lives and even things are to be treated with respect and understanding, not brutally oppressed to serve our human ends.

The ruler of the Southern Ocean was Shu, the ruler of the Northern Ocean was Hu, and the ruler of the Centre was Chaos. Shu and Hu were continually meeting in the land of Chaos, who treated them very well. They consulted together how they might repay his kindness, and said: "Men all have seven orifices for the purpose of seeing, hearing, eating and breathing, while this ruler alone has not a single one. Let us try to make them for him." Accordingly they dug one orifice in him every day. At the end of seven days Chaos died.—Chuang Tzu

In this delicately comic parable Chaos is Nature in the state of *wu-wei*—non-assertion or equilibrium. Shu and Hu are the living images of those busy persons who thought they would improve on Nature by turning dry prairies into wheat fields, and produced deserts; who proudly proclaimed the Conquest of the Air, and then discovered that they had defeated civilization; who chopped down vast forests to provide the newsprint demanded by that universal literacy which was to make the world safe for intelligence and democracy, and got wholesale erosion, pulp magazines and the organs of Fascist, Communist, capitalist and nationalist propaganda. In brief, Shu and Hu are devotees of the apocalyptic religion of Inevitable Progress, and their creed is that the Kingdom of Heaven is outside you, and in the future. Chuang Tzu, on the other hand, like all good Taoists, has no desire to bully Nature into subserving ill-considered temporal ends, at variance with the final end of men as formulated in the Perennial Philosophy. His wish is to work with Nature, so as to produce material and social conditions in which individuals may realize Tao on every level from the psychological up to the spiritual.

Compared with that of the Taoists and Far Eastern Buddhists, the Christian attitude towards Nature has been curiously insensitive and often downright domineering and violent. Taking their cue from an unfortunate remark in Genesis, Catholic moralists have regarded animals as mere things which men do right to exploit for their own ends. Like landscape painting, the humanitarian movement in Europe was an almost completely secular affair. In the Far East both were essentially religious.[4]

If we can move beyond dogmas and work with nature, then the right social conditions for everybody to realize Tao will appear. Ironically, the social morality for which Confucius yearned can only be achieved in not trying to achieve it. Social morality depends on trust and the sincere spiritual work the individual undergoes within. No dogma can set the individual, or humanity, free, because all are built on methods to induce Tao, which are methods of force.

Thus if we can be radical enough to live wu-wei, the right social and cultural conditions will emerge that will enable people to realize the Tao, and this will change our world through not striving for change. The act of trying to force change hinders change. Following your own nature is the subtle act of change. It is also the way that love transcends the personal and moves into the universal.

Our love has to exceed our boundaries to include not only our neighbors but also our enemies and the community of animals, plants, and minerals. Working with nature instead of against it is a reflection of wu-wei. Living wu-wei is thought of as one of the most difficult and, at the same time, sublime forms of spirituality that exists. Yet no matter how hard it appears to let go and trust, nothing will reveal your nature, li, more than the Tao of wu-wei. Discovering our li in turn has the power of te to inspire the world, as this is what truly brings harmony to life, Heaven to Earth.

Spiritual isolation is necessary to get to the deepest part of your being. But when your nature is revealed in this introspection, you naturally want to harmonize with the world, which corresponds to the Taoist principle of ying, mutual resonance. Li moves us out of isolation and into universal harmony, in the same way that the mystical guru of the East leaves the isolation of the cave to go back into the world. But this time the guru is you and the love you share is the love you are. The world as we know it can be anything it chooses to be, but if you do not trust the world, then the world will remain as it is. Such is the paradox of unity and our nature, wu-wei.

Notes

INTRODUCTION. THE EFFORTLESS MIND

1. Benoit, *Zen and the Psychology of Transformation,* 157–59.
2. Merton, *The Way of Chuang Tzu,* 28.
3. Radhakrishna, *Bhagavadgita,* 136.
4. Lao-tzu, *Tao Te Ching,* trans. Stephen Mitchell, chapter 1.
5. Nisbett, *The Geography of Thought,* 27.
6. Watts, *Tao: The Watercourse Way,* 5.

1. THE WAY OF NATURE IS NO IDEOLOGY OR THEOLOGY

1. Quotes.Dictionary.com   http://quotes.dictionary.com/morality_the
   _idiosyncrasy_of_decadents_with_the_ulterior.
2. Quoted in Watts, *The Way of Zen,* 26.
3. Patanjali, *The Yoga-Sutra of Patanjali,* 66.

2. THE WAY OF NATURE IS NO RELIGION OR DOGMA

1. Ouspensky, *In Search of the Miraculous,* 57–58.
2. Naimy, *The Book of Mirdad.*
3. "John Dalberg-Acton, First Baron Acton," Wikipedia; accessed July 17,
   2017; http://en.wikipedia.org/wiki/John_Dalberg-Acton,_1st_Baron
   _Acton.

4. Quoted in Chai and Chai, *The Humanist Way in Ancient China,* 331.

5. Lao-tzu, *Tao Te Ching,* chapter 18.

3. THE WAY OF THE TAO IS HARMONY

1. Chuang Tsu, *Chuang Tsu,* 29.

4. THE VIRTUE OF THE NONVIRTUOUS

1. Collins, *Light on the Path,* 16, 19.

5. PARASITIC PATTERNS OF THE UNNATURAL WORLD

1. "First Law of Thermodynamics," Wikipedia; accessed July 17, 2017; http://en.wikipedia.org/w/index.php?title=First_law_of_thermo dynamics&oldid=466893971.

2. Wilhelm, *The I Ching or Book of Changes,* 78.

6. NATURAL GOVERNMENT BORN OF TAO

1. Chuang-tzu, *Complete Works,* 114.

7. TRUST IS UNITY

1. Krishnamurti, *Krishnamurti,* 94.

2. Watts, *Way of Zen,* 170–71.

3. Chuang-tzu, *Complete Works,* 43.

8. THE PRACTICE OF YIN CULTIVATION AND THE ART OF THE SKILLFUL CRAFTSMAN

1. Lao-tzu, *Tao Te Ching,* chapter 28.

2. Lao-tzu, *Tao Te Ching,* chapter 1.

3. Quoted in Columbus and Rice, *Alan Watts,* 52–53.

4. Brendan Kelly, "Does Body Health Echo Our Planet's Climate

Crisis?" OmTimes, May 30, 2016, http://omtimes.com/2016/05/yoga
-yin-climate-crisis.

5. Quoted in Cal Newport, *Deep Work*, 143.

6. Chuang-tzu, *Complete Works*, 57–58.

7. Chuang-tzu, *Complete Works*, 50, 51.

9. SYNCHRONICITY IS THE LANGUAGE OF THE EFFORTLESS MIND

1. Maharshi, *Saddarsanam and An Inquiry into the Revelation of Truth and Oneself*, 218.

2. Quoted in James Hollis, *The Archetypal Imagination*, 57.

3. Jung, foreword to Wilhelm, *The I Ching or Book of Changes*, xxiv.

4. "Three Initiates," *The Kybalion*, 30.

5. "Three Initiates," *The Kybalion*, 35.

6. "Three Initiates," *The Kybalion*, 26.

7. Wilhelm, *The I Ching or Book of Changes*, 9.

8. Chuang Tsu, *Chuang Tsu*, 29.

10. NOTHING IS MORE USELESS THAN WU-WEI

1. Merton, *The Way of Chuang Tzu*, 153.

2. Chuang-tzu, *Complete Works*, 65.

3. Lao-tzu, *Tao Te Ching*, chapter 8.

4. Chuang-tzu, *Complete Works*, 58.

11. LIVING WU-WEI IN THE TAO OF A NEW WORLD

1. Watts, *The Joyous Cosmology*, 112.

2. Masters, *Spiritual Bypassing*, 1–2.

3. Introduction to Chuang-tzu, *Complete Works*, 5–6.

4. Huxley, *The Perennial Philosophy*, 76–77.

Bibliography

Benoit, Hubert. *Zen and the Psychology of Transformation.* Rochester, Vt.: Inner Traditions, 1990.

Blofeld, John. *Taoism: Road to Immortality.* Boston: Shambhala, 2000.

Chai, Ch'u, and Winberg Chai. *The Humanist Way in Ancient China.* New York: Bantam, 1965.

Chuang Tsu, *Chuang Tsu: Inner Chapters: A Companion to* Tao Te Ching. Translated by Gia-Fu Feng and Jane English. Portland, Ore.: Amber Lotus, 2008.

Chuang-tzu. *The Complete Works of Chuang Tzu.* Translated by Burton Watson. New York: Columbia University Press, 1968.

Cleary, Thomas. *The Taoism Reader.* Boston: Shambhala, 2012.

Collins, Mabel. *Light on the Path.* Adyar, India: Theosophical Publishing House, 1911.

Columbus, Peter J., and Donadrian L. Rice. *Alan Watts: Here and Now.* Albany: State University of New York Press, 2012.

Easwaran, Eknath, trans. *The Upanishads.* Tomales, Calif.: Nilgiri Press, 2007.

Gregory, Jason. *Enlightenment Now.* Rochester, Vt.: Inner Traditions, 2016.

———. *Fasting the Mind.* Rochester, Vt.: Inner Traditions, 2017.

———. *The Science and Practice of Humility.* Rochester, Vt.: Inner Traditions, 2014.

Hollis, James. *The Archetypal Imagination.* College Station, Tex.: Texas A&M University Press, 2002.

Huxley, Aldous. *The Perennial Philosophy.* New York: Harper Perennial, 2009.

Ivanhoe, Philip J. *The Daodejing of Laozi*. Indianapolis, Ind.: Hackett, 2003.

Ivanhoe, Philip J., and Bryan W. Van Norden. *Readings in Classical Chinese Philosophy*. Indianapolis, Ind.: Hackett, 2005.

Krishnamurti, Jiddu. *Krishnamurti: Reflections on the Self*. Chicago: Open Court, 1998.

———. *Total Freedom*. New York: Harper One, 1996.

Lao-tzu. *Tao Te Ching: An Illustrated Journey*. Translated by Stephen Mitchell. London: Frances Lincoln, 2009.

Maharshi, Sri Ramana. *Saddarsanam and An Inquiry into the Revelation of Truth and Oneself*. Translated by Nome. Santa Cruz, Calif.: Society of Abidance in Truth, 2009.

Masters, Robert Augustus. *Spiritual Bypassing*. Berkeley, Calif.: North Atlantic Books, 2010.

Merton, Thomas. *The Way of Chuang Tzu*. New York: New Directions, 2010.

Naimy, Mikhail. *The Book of Mirdad*. London: Watkins, 1999.

Needham, Joseph. *Science and Civilization in China,* vols. 1–3. Cambridge: Cambridge University Press, 1954–59.

Newport, Cal. *Deep Work*. New York: Grand Central, 2016.

Nisbett, Richard E. *The Geography of Thought*. New York: Free Press, 2004.

Ouspensky, P. D. *In Search of the Miraculous: The Teachings of G. I. Gurdjieff*. Orlando, Fla.: Harcourt, 2001.

Patanjali. *The Yoga-Sutra of Patanjali*. Translated with commentary by Chip Hartranft. Boston: Shambhala, 2003.

Ramacharaka, Yogi. *Advance Course in Yogi Philosophy and Oriental Occultism*. Chicago: Yogi Publication Society, 1931.

Reid, Daniel. *The Tao of Health, Sex, and Longevity*. New York: Simon & Schuster, 1989.

Radhakrishnan, Sarvepalli, trans. *The Bhagavadgita*. Noida, India: HarperCollins India, 2010.

Slingerland, Edward. *Trying Not to Try*. New York: Broadway Books, 2014.

Suzuki, Daisetz Teitaro, trans. *The Lankavatara Sutra: A Mahayana Text*. Philadelphia: Coronet, 1999.

Suzuki, Shunryu. *Zen Mind, Beginner's Mind*. Boston: Shambhala, 2011.

"Three Initiates." *The Kybalion: Hermetic Philosophy*. Chicago: Yogi Publication Society, 1940.

Watts, Alan. *Do You Do It, or Does It Do You?: How to Let the Universe Meditate You.* Audio CD. Louisville, Colo.: Sounds True, 2005.

———. *The Joyous Cosmology.* Novato, Calif.: New World Library, 2013.

———. *Out of Your Mind: Essential Listening from the Alan Watts Audio Archives.* Audio CD. Louisville, Colo.: Sounds True, 2004.

———. *Tao: The Watercourse Way.* New York: Pantheon, 1977.

———. *The Way of Zen.* New York: Vintage, 1999.

Welwood, John. *Perfect Love, Imperfect Relationships.* Boston: Trumpeter, 2007.

———. *Toward a Psychology of Awakening.* Boston: Shambhala, 2002.

Wilhelm, Richard. *The I Ching or Book of Changes.* Translated by Cary F. Baynes. Princeton, N.J.: Princeton University Press, 1967.

———. *The Secret of the Golden Flower: A Chinese Book of Life.* Translated by Cary F. Baynes. London: Arkana, 1984.

Wong, Eva. *Nourishing the Essence of Life.* Boston: Shambhala, 2004.

———. *Taoism: An Essential Guide.* Boston: Shambhala, 2011.

Yukteswar, Swami Sri. *The Holy Science.* Los Angeles: Self-Realization Fellowship, 1990.

Index

Page numbers in *italics* indicate illlustrations.